A MANCHESTER
MENAGERIE

TALES FROM THE URBAN JUNGLE

W0028045

Michael Beswick

Contents

The Cornerhouse has three cinema screens, three floors of galleries, a bookshop, bar and café which all provide occasional zoological connections in art, film, literature and food. A new building is under construction as HOME to Cornerhouse and the Library Theatre Company at the other end of Whitworth Street, removing both from their pivotal locations at opposite ends of Oxford Street, linking cultural centres in the City with the Universities.

*Paper Blackbird
by Lucy Gell*

*Ram in bronze resin
by Paul Smith*

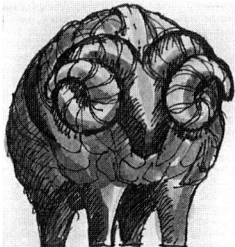

*Mechanical Dragon
in Manchester
Day Parade*

*Blue Octopus
in Manchester
Day Parade*

Foreword

Berthold Lubetkin, in his speech accepting the RIBA Gold Medal in 1982, declared that there are only four kinds of artistic activity: 'Fine art, Music, Poetry and Ornamental Pastry-making - of which Architecture is a minor branch'. Perhaps the Sugar Junction in Tib Street could create a cake to reflect the design of his Penguin Pool at the London Zoo for Manchester, decorated with fauna of the Northern Quarter, to combine the essence of Architecture and Zoology in a work of confectionery?

In the CUBE Open Art Exhibition in 2010, Emily Speed's work of miniature pieces of architecture, attached to the surfaces of a series of plaster eggs, expressed the concept of '*Egg - nest - home - country - universe*', derived from Quasimodo's relationship to the Cathedral of Notre Dame as a place of shelter which was also a defining part of who he was. We all have our identities shaped by the built environment in which we live, so these eggs establish a link between Art, Architecture and Zoology.

Whilst this is essentially a book about Manchester, it is a handbook for any city or town to help those who live there, or visit, to connect with the environment around them and with the fauna in the vernacular Urban Jungle. Some creatures will be found on the structure of buildings, others will be no more permanent than graffiti or a piece of performance poetry. Each fragment is part of a bigger picture within the frame of the built environment in which a menagerie of familiar animals often goes unnoticed, overwhelmed by a more dynamic bestiary of mythological creatures and grotesques. This zoology inspires fine architecture, art, film, drama, music, literature, folklore, commercial design - and cake decoration - in many different cultural contexts from the monumental to the ephemeral, telling a story of relationships between people and animals through scientific, social, cultural and religious symbolism. By juxtaposing seemingly unrelated subjects, extrapolating conjectural situations or simply making links by 'joining the dots' from the extremes of scarcity and plenty, private wealth and public squalor, war and peace, and all gradations in between, nothing is sacred to materialists. With a mixture of art, science, fantasy and satire, this collection of images has suggested stories which are a very personal response from a self-appointed 'zookeeper'.

Michael Beswick
The Northern Quarter, Manchester, 2014.

In the Beginning

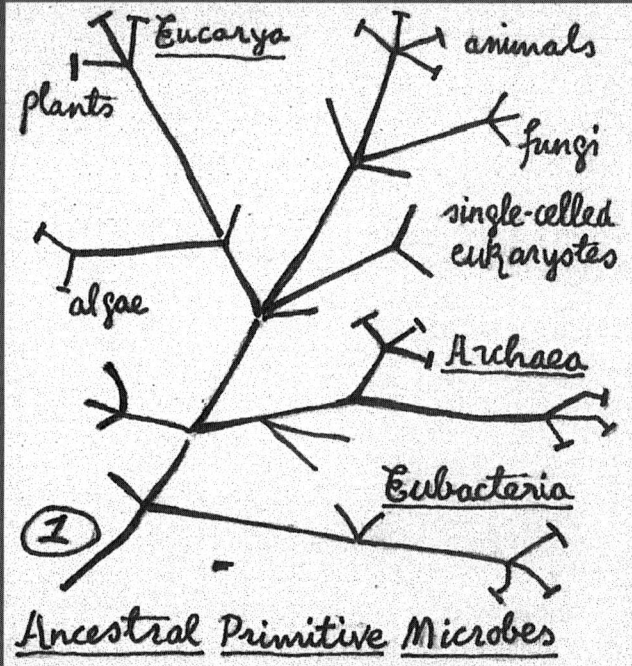

Charles Darwin observed that Natural Selection "is a power incessantly ready for action and is immeasurably superior to Man's feeble efforts as the works of Nature are to those of Art". His first iconic sketch of an evolutionary tree on the transmutation of species needed only slight adjustment to accommodate discoveries made in comparisons of DNA sequences taking our origins back to a common single-celled life form which lived in the Precambrian Period.

Once upon a time, there was a large rock hurtling in an orbit round the Sun, like an enormous chemistry set with all the elements bubbling away and reacting with each other, until two single-celled organisms collided and life, as we know it, began. As the oxygen supply increased, more complex organisms colonised the land and creatures developed which are recognisably related to today's animals. Plants appeared as a food supply which didn't run away. This satisfied the herbivores, but others were locked into maintaining a balance in a carnivorous food chain. The dinosaurs perished, for some apocalyptic reason, at the end of the Cretaceous Period but birds survived along with other life forms on land and in the sea. Then, in the last few seconds as the hands of the evolutionary clock approached midnight, Man emerged from the primeval swamps. He was bursting with arrogance and in those few seconds he created more carnage than all the natural mechanisms of evolution which had shaped the Earth and its myriad passengers throughout its entire development.

Most animals led relatively simple lives with limited horizons in which to raise their young, catch their food and find shelter, but Man had opposable thumbs, stood on two legs and grew brain cells which he quickly employed to exploit the resources he found in his environment. He developed a means of communication and began to paint graphic scenes on the walls of the caves in which he lived, thereby establishing story-telling as an art form. Animals featured prominently in these prehistoric paintings, and the format was stable for thousands of years, indeed, the illustrations at Chauvet were made over a period of 5000 years in the same cave using the same techniques. As the human population increased, the cerebral evolution of Man caused his path to diverge from that of other animal life forms which evolved physically rather than mentally. Consequently, Man survived the last Ice Age and became the dominant land animal who began to put everything else at risk. Even if the dinosaurs had still existed, it is doubtful that their formidable size would have tilted the balance in their favour because, faced with the predations of Man, they would have had no defence which might have given them a chance to develop into something 'modern', as some of the smaller animals have done. Man assumed 'dominion' over all other life forms. The elite Shaman class of that primitive society quickly discovered the advantage of inventing gods in their own image and found that, by appointing themselves as intermediaries, it was also possible to assume 'dominion' over their fellow men. After a disastrous flood, they persuaded their brethren that they had made a covenant with those gods who had instructed them to replenish the Earth. It would be their sons who would strike fear into every beast, every fowl and every fish. Having achieved spectacular success in this project, Man went on to select passages from Genesis to justify European colonisation of the world, the slave trade and to exploit his fellow Men and their resources within a 'dominion' of fear.

The illiterate peasant classes were kept in ignorance and given only simple images to illustrate Biblical stories, so the wood carvings in Manchester Cathedral follow the same story-telling tradition as the cave paintings. Both have much to say about the craftsmen who made closely observed records of the world about them through the representation of animals aesthetically, practically and, occasionally, ironically. This tradition was the forerunner of the printed word - and written satire.

Following various episodes of enlightenment, the colonies were given back to their indigenous populations.   However, the power to exploit them passed from missionaries and merchant adventurers to global organisations who continued to plunder the natural resources, the animals and the people, destroying more of the environment. Man's carnage began to accelerate at an alarming rate and, whilst it was possible to identify plants and animals which they knew were endangered, scientists believed that unknown species were disappearing faster than they were able to discover them because scientists don't know what they don't know. Trusted academics were preoccupied in pursuing research which would make nature 'useful' or 'relevant' but were not concerned that specimens were killed in order to analyse and categorise them until problems arose when they used live animals for their experiments. The dried and stuffed specimens held in the collections of academic institutions would eventually become the only point of contact humans would ever have with many species.   Then they found that the institutions themselves were endangered! Under severe financial pressure, their academic science was reduced to the point of trivialisation as they tried to maintain their credibility in the context of the alien commercial activities in which they were embedded. Whilst it was no longer politically fashionable to harm animals in the name of vital medical research, no-one seemed to recognise that it was equally barbaric to destroy their natural habitat through the commercial exploitation of all manner of resources, thereby displacing indigenous communities, distorting local economies and endangering even more species. Their short-term policies to maximise profits made them forget the moral lesson from the childhood tale of the man who killed the goose that laid golden eggs.

The fine line between art and science was examined in the 'Interspecies' exhibition at the Cornerhouse in 2009. The film by Nicolas Primat interacting with tribes of bonobo apes, and Rachel Mayeri's 'Primate Cinema' with actors cast as primates, demonstrated that humans have more in common with their primate relatives than they might wish to admit. In art, this is not a problem but, in applied science, two films in 2011, showed how the dire effects of exploitation could lead to unintended consequences. 'Project Nim' was a documentary which examined a hippy linguistic experiment of the 1970s to bring up an infant chimpanzee in a human family to investigate the possibility of communicating with another species. Nim was smart enough to learn how to exploit humans but he was not able to detach himself from his natural chimpanzee behaviour, so the humans had to abandon their experiment. This resulting bad science caused his return to the institution which had raised his mother for the purpose of medical testing, but he was 'rescued' to become a lone chimpanzee in a donkey sanctuary! He was joined by other chimpanzees when the testing facility was shut down and, having lived all his life in alien environments, he spent his twilight years enjoying the company of his own kind. Questionable experimenting on animals in the name of medical science was the background of 'The Rise of the Planet of the Apes' where the experiments got out of hand and inevitable spectacular chaos followed rapidly. This was a cautionary tale for those who had assumed dominion over animals but had not accepted that the sacrifice of those animals in the cause of research amounted to commercial exploitation of the creatures in the pursuit of obscene profits, putting the benefits to human health into second place and pushing the welfare of the animals off the scale.

When Man began to take communications more seriously, he left evidence of his history. The alabaster funerary jar from 1100BC in the collection of the City Art Gallery would have been a message to the Baboon-faced deity, Hapy, to guard the entrails of a deceased person to aid their mummified carcass to live on with the gods in the afterlife. Artefacts from the Egyptology department of the Manchester Museum assembled in their 'Unearthed' exhibition included cosmetic dishes in the form of fishes and ducks, designs which have been repeated in one style or another up to the present day. The wooden Horse on wheels demonstrated that children's toys have hardly changed since the time of the Pharaohs. Walter Klemenz, a German prisoner of war working on a farm in Kent during the Second World War, followed the same pattern using available materials to make his articulated Dog, whether to send for his own children or to amuse those on the farm, we don't know. This was one of the artefacts in the Imperial War Museum North exhibition 'Once upon a Wartime' about novels for children on their experiences of war. Toys which depend on a child's imaginative involvement have been superseded by the virtual images which can be manipulated on a small screen by pressing buttons, creating a different sort of dependency.

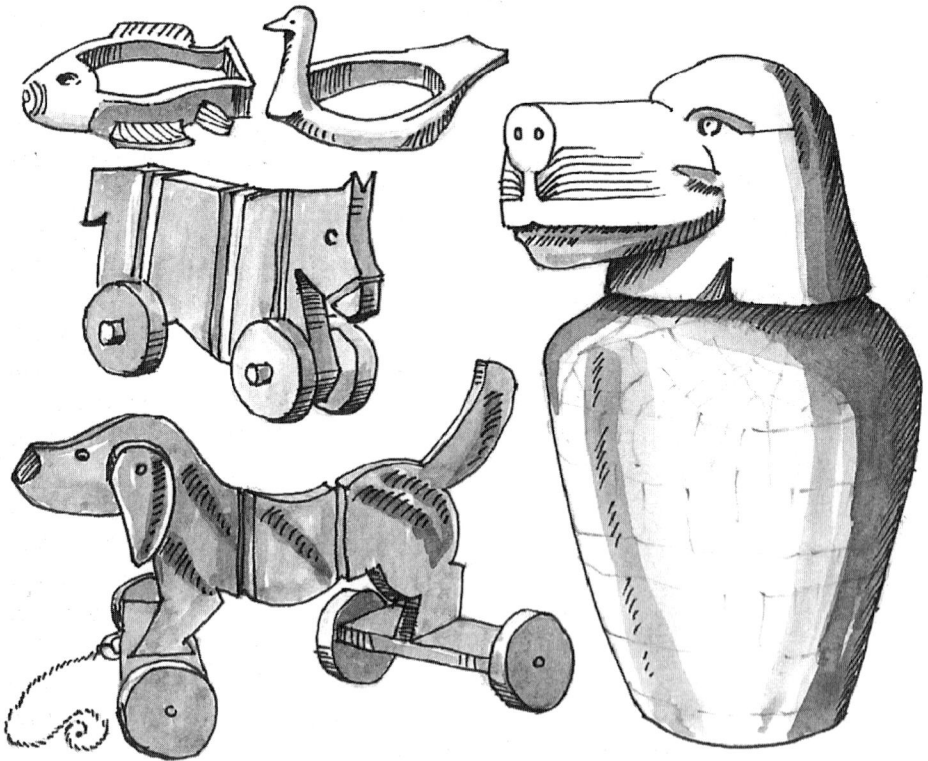

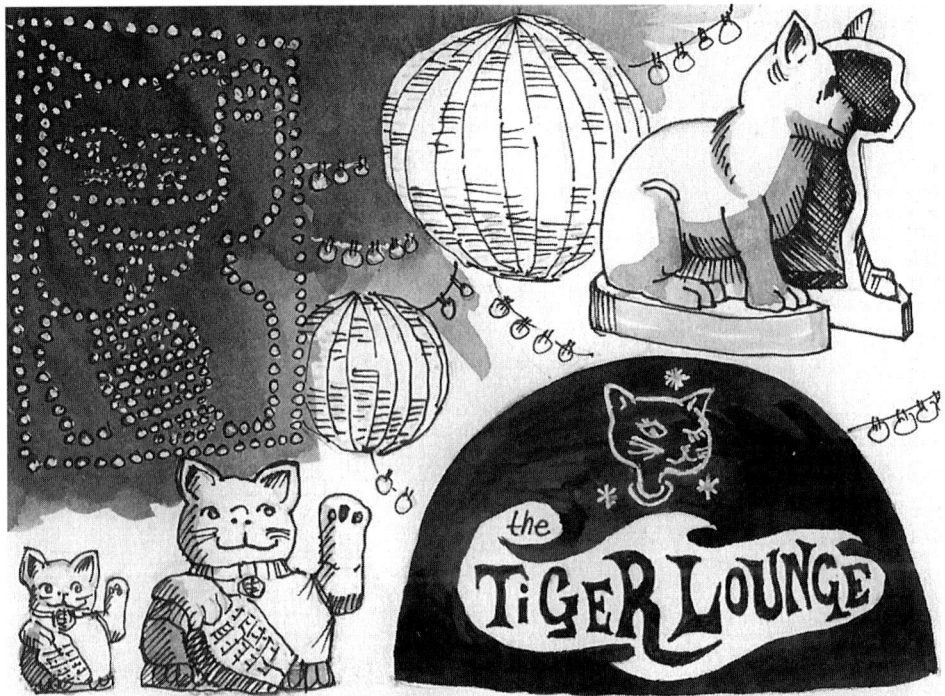

In a settled society, some animals became domesticated and Cats took advantage of the situation, training human beings so that the ancient Egyptians would venerate them in recognition of this magical ability. A wooden coffin in the form of a Cat, on display in the '*Unearthed*' exhibition, would have held the mummified body of the animal which had presumably passed into the care of the Cat-headed goddess, Bast. This Egyptian reverence gave rise to classical legends from which medieval church leaders derived their own 'familiar spirits', slaves in the form of Cats which attended a witch or a warlock and were therefore demons in disguise. Satan, whose favourite form was a Black Cat, exploited this familiarity, adding a darker dimension to its character. Spiteful women are supposed to fight like Cats, or make the same hideous noise perhaps? Cat-burglars denigrate the species at the same time as celebrating its agility and stealth. More positive images of mechanical Cats inhabit shop windows around Chinatown, their arms waving to bring us good luck - and to tempt us into the stores. Cats were made 'cool' by popular jazz musicians in the 1940s, a connection taken up by the Tiger Lounge with a name evoking the thrill of big game-hunting which paradoxically is expressed in a stylised Cool pussy Cat emblem with a saucy wink and a promise to make 'Cat Music for Cat People'. The fiery background to their logo also conjures up hints of Satanic connections? What a complex creature is the Cat, to have such a history.

In the Middle Ages, the Church controlled education and took the opportunity to use the decoration on their buildings as a visual aid to celebrate God and all the creatures He had created for the benefit of an illiterate population. The craftsmen, charged with carrying out the task of illustrating this concept, took their inspiration from the world around them and the plants and animals on the misericords in Manchester Cathedral were represented in natural detail but left much to the imagination in the contextual significance of the images. Some were pure religious symbols but others were irreverent or ironic gestures against the establishment. 17th century details on the Shakespeare pub show characters from village life, including a fool riding a pig and waving an inflated bladder on a stick. The rustic charm of English folklore surfaces from time to time when Morris dancers gather in St Ann's Square. Education became more universal as movable type made books cheaper, so people were able to read their Bible in English, but illustrations were still used to reinforce the text on the printed page. Introduction to zoology in the primary school was through 'nature study', and stuffed animals would have been something magical to inner city school children. In the reconstruction of a 1920s classroom in the Portland Basin Museum, a symbolic goose sits on the book cupboard, keeping one eye on the children and the other on the classroom clock. Sadly, these visual aids have been replaced by modern technical wizardry which children carry around in their pockets - with none of the magic.

Victorian antiquarians revived medieval craftsmanship to celebrate God and nature in an attempt to restore the connection between the Church and the community with familiar visual imagery, but the population was becoming more enlightened by nonconformist chapels where there was little or no decoration. Manual decoration of buildings struggled on into the 20th century with the Arts and Crafts movement competing with machine-made components for the construction industry. Terracotta details at the Manchester School of Art interpret medieval carvings in Art Nouveau scrolls with owls, hedgehogs, mice, other small animals and birds inhabiting entwined foliage around the capitals of piers in the Holden Gallery. Applied decoration was no longer affordable after the Great War and the plain surfaces of Modern Architecture were an economic expression of a new World Order trying to make sense of austerity - a cycle which is currently repeating itself, hopefully without resorting to war? The celebration of animals would survive by other means. Art and drama assumed more prominence in the kaleidoscope of creative activity and the Library Theatre's production of 'Cell' told the story of a young man who sealed himself and his *alter ego* into the darkness of his bedroom and became obsessed with the natural history of the Arctic Tern which, paradoxically, sees more daylight than any other creature on the planet as a result of its migratory patterns.

The preoccupation with animals in literature began with Aesop, not a Shaman but a Phrygian slave of the 6th century BC. He was the accredited author of fables, some recycled from ancient Egyptian papyri, and adopted the device of anthropomorphism which people accepted as children. They did not appreciate that Aesop had burdened the animals with some very undesirable human attributes in order to demonstrate Man's frailties, so the animals became endowed with fabricated habits which did not reflect their own temperaments. Aesop had unwittingly created a minefield of misdirection in communications, with no idea that these false stereotypes could become logos to enhance the reputations of commercial organisations. A walk down New Cathedral Street is an object lesson in marketing which could have been designed by Aesop himself. Jean René Lacoste's nickname in the 1920s was 'The Crocodile' because of his tenacity on the tennis court so, like many successful sportsmen, he exploited his popularity and made this device the logo for his range of sports clothing and merchandise. Ted Baker's lettering sprouting Deer antlers, evoked the 'call of the wild' in their outdoor clothing, but their grotesque animated Christmas turkey did not spare the feelings of the naked bird! Radley's rugged and faithful Scottish Terrier logo had nothing at all to do with the lasting quality of their clothing but was the beloved pet of the company's designer. Louis Vuitton's diamond-patterned pantomime elephant stretched the imagination as the 16th century Italian Harlequin and his sweetheart, Columbine, were supposedly invisible to all but each other, but as the elephant 'disappears' against a similar diamond-patterned background, an expensive handbag stands out prominently.

Behind all these shop windows and logos, there was another world inside the prestigious stores whose amazing displays of merchandise would have stretched the imagination of Aesop. He would have been baffled by a collection of giant plaster icons featuring a goldfish, a squirrel, a budgerigar, a snail, a rocking horse and a panel of six low relief horses heads amongst the fashions of Harvey Nichols and might have created a new collection of fables around them? The zoological hint of a theme demanded a deeper meaning in case there could be other tenuous connections which were not immediately obvious? Rocking horses, pet budgerigars and goldfish could have evoked pleasurable childhood memories, and the sight of a squirrel always generated some excitement. Snails raised more unpleasant images of little girls being tortured by sibling brothers intent on some personal vendetta. More mature lady gardeners have been known to pursue their own vendettas against slimy creatures which demolish their precious seedlings, whether this be snails or boys of any age. The horses heads in inappropriate places conjured up more sinister forms of vendetta. But what had any of this to do with fashion? The display designer claimed that they did not follow the practice of 'joining dots' and had no need to make sense of anything. Their prime objective was to be 'different'. Who could have failed to notice that?

Medieval shops expressed their individuality by hanging outside a display of articles available for sale inside but as stock multiplied, lettering took over this function, 'multi-tasking' with a vocabulary of images including animals, thanks to Aesop. The Owl was the emblem of Athene, goddess of wisdom, patron of arts and trades and protector of Athens. Owls on coins of ancient Greece meant that 'sending owls to Athens', had the same meaning as the English 'carrying coals to Newcastle', in recognition of the economic power of the city. The City Art Gallery's press-moulded glass jar made by Matthew Turnbull of Sunderland in 1888, characterises both the power and the wisdom of the Owl. The Jobwise Owl logo links their name to the legendary wisdom of the bird, but using this image to enhance their reputation could possibly amount to a form of identity theft? Coyotes Club uses this technique in an inspired piece of typography to give their establishment a slightly dangerous edge by linking it to a predatory prairie wolf which needs to be taken seriously - not like Looney Tunes' hapless Wiley Coyote?

The austerity of British architecture since the end of the First World War has presented an irresistible challenge to graffiti artists to create 'affordable' decoration on blank walls. To some their work is an act of vandalism, to others it adds an essential detail to innoculate the environment against sterile corporate images. The Jaguar leaping out to prey on passers-by in Deansgate resembles figures mounted on the bonnets of expensive motor cars? Such graffiti intrigues the uninitiated as nothing in the neighbourhood relates to the image - except a passing youth with the same logo on an up-market Puma hoodie? Are corporate logos on the products of fashion houses nothing more than guerilla advertising?

Mass communications saturate people's awareness of their environment with myriad images which require sophisticated decoding, if not with some technology then certainly with some intelligence. Survival on a dying planet depends on the ability to create a sustainable ecosystem to balance the depredations of global corporations who plunder scarce resources believing that they will last forever. Conservationists recycle materials to avoid these consequences and in some communities this has become a way of life because they have never had access to resources of any sort. In the Whitworth Gallery, a colourful hooked rag rug by Louisa Creed sends a message for the future that we must conserve our resources along with our vital craft skills, exploiting a wide range of colours, patterns and textures of materials which would have been abandoned in this throw-away society. To sustain us in a cold abstract world which is driving itself into a desperate situation from which it may never recover, the image of the Armadillo on the rug reinforces the message through the voice of the animals, but is anyone listening?

Inevitably, there will be animals which have not been included here as this collection is not intended to be an exhaustive gazetteer of zoological Manchester. Everyone is invited to fill in the gaps from their own experiences or be encouraged to look around and be prepared to be surprised by what they had never noticed before and be ready to respond to ephemeral experiences. Medieval alchemists, in their quest to make gold or eternal life, explored the ancient Greek concepts of the four elements of Earth, Water, Air and Fire, represented by four Platonic solids shaping their atoms as tetrahedron, cube, octahedron and dodecahedron. Their philosophy is rooted in mathematical concepts and can be a starting point to investigate how these four environments, in which animals flourish, have been expressed in fine art, music, poetry and ornamental pastry-making. We might discover that they all have their own stories. Are you sitting comfortably?

In the shadow of the Beetham Tower, one of the tallest buildings in England, the White Lion pub in Liverpool Road makes its own statement with a pair of statuesque beasts guarding the doors as if it were a Chinese temple.

EARTH
WATER
AIR
FIRE

The Lion's Tale

A Lion paperweight in pressed blue opaline glass, made by John Derbyshire of Salford around 1874, is part of the Manchester Collection in the City Art Gallery. This animal is more relaxed than the more formal classic pose which occurs throughout art history, from the Sphinx of ancient Egypt to the bronze Lions which Sir Edwin Landseer added to the base of Nelson's Column in London's Trafalgar Square in 1867.

Man would have you believe that he was given 'dominion' over all the Animals, but he learned the hard way that I was King of the Jungle but I'm not so sure about the Urban Jungle. Why they call that a 'jungle' is beyond my comprehension. Even the jungle of my natural Kingdom isn't as jungly as you might imagine. Lions live on open plains where they can keep an eye on anything that moves, not in a sweaty rainforest where you don't know what might drop out of the next tree! So my great-grandfather, taking the job as King of Belle Vue Zoo, must have thought it was somewhat beneath him. The owners had taken a lot of trouble to put such a wide variety of animals on display and made sure that they were all well looked after. But visitors had no appreciation of this and thought the zoo was a medieval deer park and animals were 'fair game'. It wasn't a game! Oh, dear me, no. Ladies insisted on carrying parasols to protect them from the sun. This is Manchester, so when do they expect the sun to shine? I know what they needed the parasols for. To them, animals were not interesting unless they made a noise or chased each other. But if that turned into a mating ritual, those prim and proper ladies had a fit of the vapours and complained about 'indecency'. They didn't appreciate that poking a parasol through the bars would start a perfectly natural chain of events. The closing concert in Piccadilly Gardens for the 'We Face Forward' celebration of West African art included a handsome dancer wearing a splendid cloak decorated with my portrait. Now, that's what I call appreciation.

They were supposed to be learning about animal behaviour, forgetting that it was human beings who started the war that caused Belle Vue Zoo to be taken over by the military authorities as a barrage balloon base which, perversely, made it more of a target. The Emergency Committee got excited in case the gardens were bombed and wild animals escaped. They gave the keepers rifles and drew up a list of all the big cats and a few bears to be shot on sight - summary justice, I think that's called. Snakes were expected to perish in the cold so there must have been a lot of people praying for a hard winter in case they disappeared into the shrubbery. It wasn't us they needed to worry about, it was the two-legged animals dropping bombs who were the real problem. They cancelled the band concerts and the firework displays, so life became a bit Spartan, but the zoo's greatest difficulty was food shortages: no bananas, no birdseed, green-dyed horsemeat for the real carnivores, not much fish so sea-lions had to eat beef soaked in cod liver oil. Air raids cut off the heating so we lost a lot of tropical fish, a few exotic birds and some young animals who weren't acclimatised. They took in animals from other zoos and the local people wanted them to look after their pets. Some of those would have made good supplements to our wartime diet. Most of the animals survived, but it's a wonder that we didn't all finish up as pet food? After the war, things picked up and the collection was soon as comprehensive as that in the London Zoo. By the 1960s finance was getting tight so breeding and replacement of animals slowed down. They made extra money by providing quarantine facilities for importers, but zoos became 'old-fashioned' when the 'Safari Park' was invented. If they'd wanted monkeys to cause havoc with radio aerials on cars we could have arranged that without their having to drive through. Some animals appeared on television which had been invented so that people could be entertained at home, devaluing an outing to the zoo which was no longer a treat because it couldn't compete with the new technology. Eventually the zoo closed and all the other amusements shut down. Now there's hardly any reason to leave home for anything and people live in self-inflicted isolation worse than animals in a zoo. It's all a question of economics. We don't have problems like that in the jungle, so I take it personally when my image gets used to promote 'Donkey Stones': cheap blocks of limestone, bleach and cement. The mixture was originally designed for textile mills to make non-slip surfaces on stone staircases when rubbed on with a little water. It wasn't long before house-proud women found they were good for making their front doorsteps look like new. Eli Whalley of Ashton-under-Lyne chose a 'Lion' as his brand trademark in 1891 because it reminded him of visits to Belle Vue as a child. I don't understand the connection because he couldn't have seen too many ladies scrubbing doorsteps in the zoo. I wish great-grandfather could have eaten him along with young Albert and his stick with its *'orses 'ead 'andle*?

But there they are, in the Portland Basin Museum, the stones and the moulds in which they were made. Even that fellow Aesop might have thought a Donkey would have been a more obvious brand image than a Lion? Now, to put my picture on a vehicle, so I can be driven around to be admired, is much more appropriate to my status. Customisation is a very fashionable form of advertisement so images of majestic animals like me set the right tone for the Vehicle and Fleet Graphics firm. Sky Television vans covered with big game animals are mobile hoardings to advertise their regular series of nature films about the animals - not, I trust, to encourage people to go Big Game hunting? A zoo in a box, I suppose you might call it, but I don't know who watches the programmes any more. They all seem to have machines to do that for them while they're all busy doing something else. Don't they realise that if they store 500 hours of films, it takes 500 hours to watch them? If they manage to clock up a full box they obviously had better things to do, so they're not likely to find the time to watch them anyway. They talk so much about multitasking but if they subcontract their amusement to a viewing machine they seem to have missed the point, so if they insist on doing two things at the same time, they can't be doing either of them properly. Perhaps that's the value of the machine? Human behaviour is a complete mystery to me. But I digress.

Where was I? Ah, yes, economics which some people believe is a science but it really is no better informed than divination by reading tea leaves or rummaging around in some poor deceased animal's innards. Let's face it, a good financial crisis is just an excuse to say that there's no money to feed the Lions. Lions don't eat money, but if I did what comes naturally and ate them or their pets, I'd be labelled heartless or savage. If I'm hungry, I'll eat whatever I can catch. That's what Lions do! I don't get sentimental about what I eat. People never think about these things when they take us out of our natural habitat to bring us to this very unforgiving climate and put us in cages where there's no food 'on the hoof', as you might say. They brought one of my distant cousins and his wife over from Tunis in 1840. I'm surprised they had the sense not to separate them. They put them in the London Zoo but his wife had an accident and died, so he just pined away and died a few weeks later. But that wasn't the end of his story. There was an artist, Sir Edwin Landseer, who painted animals in great detail and he found it a lot safer to paint them if they were dead. He made a portrait of my cousin and called the picture '*The Desert*' which said more about the background than the subject, so it was retitled '*The Fallen Monarch*' which was much more appropriate. It hangs in the City Art Gallery for all to see. They've got another picture of a cousin-once-removed, Cheetah, with a stag and two Indians - from India, that is - painted by George Stubbs in 1765. Cheetah had been given to King George III by George Pigot, the Governor of Madras who gave him to his uncle the Duke of Cumberland, the Ranger at Windsor, who also kept a menagerie. All these aristocrats seem to have rampaged around the world collecting anything that took their fancy.

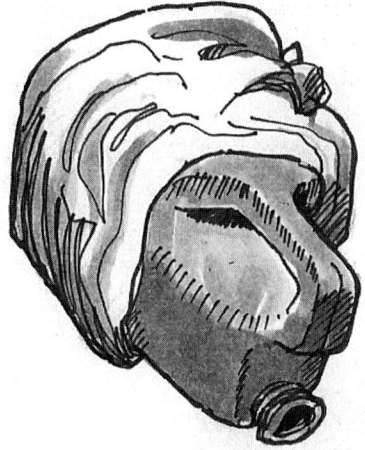

There were so many of those aristocrats and big game hunters that they kept Van Ingens' taxidermy business going throughout the 20th century preparing over 2000 Tigers for their customers. For one month's entertainment every year, the King of Nepal's guests managed to shoot an average of 55 Tigers, 13 Leopards, 8 Rhinos and 3 Bears, although Goldilocks seems to have taken no part in this carnage. In pursuit of such 'entertainment', it's hardly surprising that Tigers are endangered! Before conservation was invented, Zoos were supposed to have an educational purpose as well as to display live animals for entertainment but scientists, studying animals for their research, insisted on killing their specimens to find out what made them tick - by which time, they'd stopped ticking! They said that their object was to advance knowledge of zoology and animal physiology. Now, I know you can't make omelettes without breaking eggs, but they were cutting and carving their way through the animal kingdom like they were preparing for a barbeque. Empire-builders saw everything in their colonies as a means to make profit, exploiting food, minerals, even people. They sent in their Holy Men as missionaries to explain that their God had given them dominion over the fish of the sea, the fowl of the air, the cattle and every creeping thing that creepeth upon the earth, so any local gods would have to go as there was only One God. Theirs! It's somewhat ironic, then, that Empires gave way to privatised globalisation as masters of financial power. The 'We Face Forward' exhibition at the City Art Gallery included pieces by Romuald Hazoumè from Benin who said "I send back to the West that which belongs there, the refuse of a consumer society that invades Africa every day" as his observation on the continuum of imperialisation and consumerism in the context of Africa's changing position within the global economy. His African masks, made from discarded plastic containers, took on a very feline form like indigenous carvings, particularly the piece called 'Sénégauloise'.

As well as the commercialisation of animals in the wild, merchants exploit their images by putting ceramic models of Big Cats amongst displays to make the fashions look exotic rather than just expensive! At least, they no longer use real animal skins like cave-men who had none of the options that are available today. The organisations which shout very loud about animal rights banished mink stoles to the pawn shop or the equivalent they've reconstructed in Portland Basin Museum. But it's alright to recycle them in art installations in places like the Victoria Baths, I suppose. It's beyond my comprehension that women could bear to wrap a whole animal skin, complete with arms and legs and head, around their necks when they run a mile from a live animal? Same problem that Landseer had, I suppose, they had to be dead first - the animals, that is? Those fine artists were preoccupied with classical themes and John William Godward's painting called 'Expectation', in 1900, evokes the mythical Greek Sphinx which had the head of a Woman, body and paws of a Lion, wings of a Bird and tail of a Serpent. He couldn't get all the relevant bits so he settled for a decadent Woman on a Tiger Skin! I hope the City Art Gallery appreciates that?

We must accept it as a form of flattery when artists and designers copy our natural patterns as decoration. These are not accidental and Alan Turing tried to explain the variations in terms of mathematics and chemistry. He called that morphogenesis. I wonder what people are hiding from when they camouflage themselves like animals? The more enterprising *fashionistas* create artificial alternatives to make it socially acceptable to be seen in clothes which are not 'real'. Harvey Nichols' display themed on the *'Urban Jungle'* featured animal figures in natural poses but constructed from a variety of strange materials like small wooden blocks with holes to represent Leopard spots, mirror-coated plastics textured like Crocodile skin. Mulberry in Spinningfields filled their windows with families of inflated Zebras but their handbags had no stripes whatsoever! More designers wanting to be different, I suppose? So how does a ceramic Leopard wearing an up-market silk tie add value to the merchandise in Hilfiger's window?

Because so many animals have been hunted or poached almost to oblivion, the academics have parted company from the missionaries and have their own 'Mission Statement' which sets out to 'manage' species by promoting biodiversity to 'rescue' those which they have endangered. I think that's called 'job creation'? When they talk about preserving things, I have nightmares of being turned into Lion Jam. The thought of being released back into the wild doesn't appeal to an old cynic like me. We've become institutionalised in the zoo because the wild out there doesn't exist as we knew it. Are they going to replant the jungle? And if they could do that, how long before somebody chops it down again to make furniture or palm oil before they get the chance to fill it up with animals? Noah was lucky because he didn't have a problem with opportunists when the land dried out. Even Rhinos couldn't defend themselves against the idiots who believed that Marco Polo thought they were Unicorns. The theory up until then was that they could only be caught if they were found nestling in the lap of a virgin. Can you see a virgin willing to let an ugly beast like a Rhino get up close and personal? I don't think so. A live Rhino is not cuddly like a dead Mink! But people still think that their horns are an aphrodisiac or have magical medicinal properties. That's how they got endangered in the first place because they can't reproduce when they've been killed for their horns. People never learn! If they release Rhinos back into the wild it's a bit like breeding Grouse to populate the moors for gunmen to massacre. That's 'conservation'. Real Rhinos are at risk because they're too ugly for any established religion - or anybody else for that matter - to want a spiritual attachment to them. They will soon be no more than a memory and children will never understand that the logos on traffic barriers mean, paradoxically, that they are as tough as old Rhinos. The barriers are blessed by the Health and Safety Regulations which are venerated much more than any religious tract.

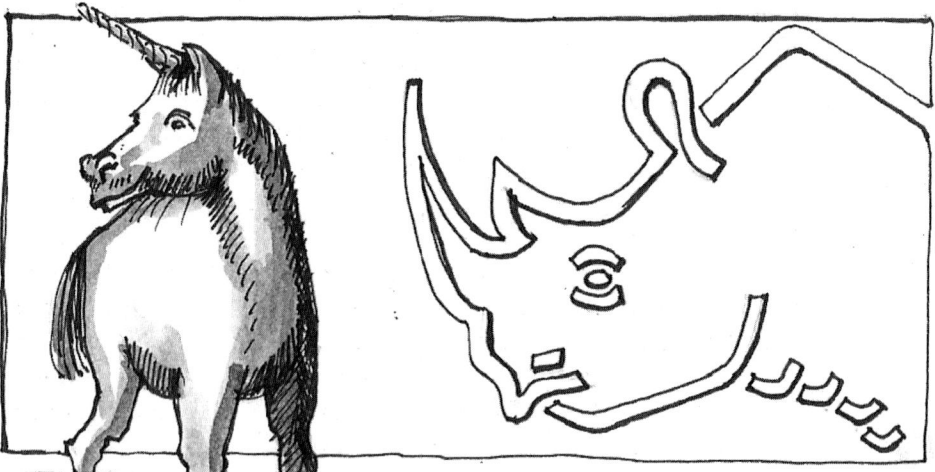

And while we're on the subject of Unicorns, my relationship with that ostentatious creature goes back to King James VI of Scotland who became James I of England, uniting the crowns of the two Kingdoms in 1603. He made a few adjustments to the royal heraldry and, quite properly, retained the Lion as the dexter supporter of England, with its history going right back to the Normans. He brought with him one of the Unicorn supporters of Scotland to replace the sinister Red Dragon of Wales. The pair of Royal Beasts outside a smart restaurant in Mount Street bear the Royal Shield with English Lions *passant gardant*, Scottish Lion *rampant* - and an Irish Harp *silent*. That Welsh Dragon must have done something unspeakably sinister to have been air-brushed out of heraldic history? The restaurant, by the way, had started life as a Tax Office and the Royal Beasts were a statement of the authority of the Crown. Not like the helium balloons you see in Market Street, with a human somewhere underneath, hanging on to all the strings, tethered to inflated images of modern merchandising. So the rather handsome Lion is obliged to rub shoulders with a pink Unicorn. Pink, indeed!? Amongst all the strange characters from children's comics or cartoon films, I'm sure the Lion and Unicorn are not intended to represent the Crown? You must always be aware of the company you keep. But if your image is to be put about, there's no such thing as bad publicity?

31

In the days when the zoo was still acquiring new animals, great-grandfather's Kingdom was always expanding and it must have felt very much like home when four Giraffes arrived. They caused quite a stir amongst the ladies who all wanted dresses to match their patterns, although I have no idea why ladies wanted to disguise themselves as Giraffes? In spite of being as tall as a tree, four Giraffe skins wouldn't go far. However, it was not their patterns but their unusual form which inspired furniture makers. The City Gallery has a cabinet designed by Roger Fry around 1915 and made by John Joseph Kallenborn in the Omega Workshops with decoration of a pair of Giraffes as shapes inlaid in hardwood marquetry patterns similar to Cubist collages. Then in 1924 Stella Crofts made a ceramic piece of a group of Giraffes, with their long necks entwined and their decorative patterns painted by hand, exploiting all the characteristics of these unique animals. She made a similar piece of a family of Zebras.

It's satisfying to see artists and craftsmen worshipping so many of my subjects, finding different aspects to inspire their work, not just the colours, patterns and textures of their skins, but something to relate to their character or their origins - a bit of old-fashioned symbolism. The unusual carvings of Kangaroos on the 'poppy heads' of the Cathedra, the Bishop's chair in Manchester Cathedral, commemorate the appointment of the third Bishop in 1886 from his post as Bishop of Melbourne in Australia. The Collegiate Church did not become the Cathedral until 1847 and had no need for a Cathedra until then, so a new item of furniture was made in best Gothic Revival style which was fashionable at the time. Medieval craftsmen were in the habit of altering buildings and fittings in the fashion of the day, so I wonder if making a fake medieval piece of furniture just to change it into something most unmedieval reflects the same spirit - or might that be seen as cultural vandalism?

Many species have been put at risk through Man's exploitation, corruption, ignorance and superstition which are far more difficult to deal with than the trivia of ephemeral fashions. People's grand ideas about habitat management develop ecotourism to give the wildlife an economic value but this is a compromise rather than leaving things to nature. It's always difficult to maintain a balance between wild creatures and their human neighbours who trade illegal bits of animals to buy guns for warlords in the name of 'poverty relief'. It's like herding Cats, and Big Cats like me like to be seen but not herded. We Lions have our Pride!

Elephant in the Room

The baby Asian Elephant in the Living Worlds Gallery of
Manchester Museum came from Belle Vue Zoo where it
had died naturally and was bought as a specimen in
1946. The Museum has taken on Belle Vue's role and
is registered as a Zoo in order to keep its collection of
live animals in its Vivarium.

That gossipy Lion might think he's King of the Zoo, but the Zoo would have no credibility without me. Elephants have what is called 'presence'. Belle Vue opened its collection to the public some ten years before the Royal Zoological Society's Regent Park Zoo in London and it was run for a hundred years by the Jennison family who introduced progressive methods of animal welfare and acquired many unusual and rare animals. Maharajah was an eight year-old Indian Elephant who became a legend. He was one of the zoo's early acquisitions, bought for £680 in 1872 by James Jennison from a travelling circus in Edinburgh. It was intended that he should make the journey to Manchester by train but Maharajah didn't like that idea and demolished the railway wagon which was to transport him. So he was led by his keeper, Lorenzo Lawrence, the two hundred miles on foot in ten days. A painting by Heywood Hardy in the City Art Gallery shows an incident of a 'Disputed Toll' on this epic journey. The story itself is a disputed urban myth, but it was feasible because the walk had been made necessary when the animal destroyed its rail transport. Maharajah lived at the zoo for ten years and was one of several Elephants who were major performers throughout its existence. When the zoo was being run down in the 1970s, animals were sold to other zoos, private collectors - and a travelling circus - until there was only one Elephant left. She, like Maharajah, did not approve of the idea of taking a train to Rotterdam, or anywhere else, but before another long walk could be arranged she suffered pneumonia and heart failure and had to be shot. So 1979 saw the end of the Belle Vue collection.

Roger Oldham, a local architect and lecturer, was a regular visitor to Belle Vue and he took a different view from that of the man who made Donkey Stones. His drawings in the collection of the City Art Gallery show that the zoo was an inspiration to him when he made his 'Manchester Alphabet' in 1906. He quite naturally selected Belle Vue to represent 'Z', so what image did he select to illustrate 'Zoo'? He wasn't influenced by all the bluster of that pompous Lion, oh no. He picked the animal without which there really would have been no zoo, the Elephant! As I said before, Elephants have presence and live animals are often surprising to small children who discover that their toys, cartoon films and picture books have little in common with the real thing. Contact with the animals in Belle Vue was valuable to their understanding of the creatures and a ride on the Elephant was the highlight of their visit. When poor Maharajah died, he was reduced to a skeleton - too big a job for the taxidermist, I suppose. It was on display in the small museum at the zoo until it was sold to the Manchester Museum where it is now the centrepiece of the Manchester Gallery.

Z for ZOO

Belle Vue it is true
Is a very good Zoo,
Brass bands and rip-raps
And set pieces too,
Are part of the programme
At Manchester Zoo.

Reproduced by permission of Manchester City Art Gallery

The cabinets surrounding Maharajah's bones hold a collection of artefacts made from ivory. As you can see from Hardy's picture, his tusks had been cut short and between their truncated ends they had fixed a metal bar to which children could cling, to be lifted off the ground by the Elephant. Children these days are not even allowed to swing from trees, so I don't know how they would respond to swinging from a real live Elephant? Health and Safety Regulations would not approve. The bar has gone and the worn ends of the tusks are now supported by metal rings on rods fixed to the floor. The Benin carvings give an idea of how big an Elephant's tusks can grow. These are three or four hundred years old and the decoration records incidents from the life of the Oba, the ruler of Benin, showing details of legends and religious ceremonies. They were 'captured' by a British naval expedition in 1897, but today, Customs Officers at Manchester Airport 'capture' illegal items from tourists who still don't understand that animals die because of their ivory and will continue to do so if people are prepared to pay for ivory products. It's an uphill battle when there's money involved, I can tell you!

The Museum holds a collection of small models based on archeological remains of beasts which became extinct long before zoologists were invented. These include Tertiary Elephants, small pig-like animals with a prehensile lip which developed as a snout to become the trunk of the Quaternary Elephants from the Pleistocene Period. They had prominent teeth for excavating food and these grew into tusks. The Quaternary Elephants, which resemble modern animals, include the Wooly Mammoth, *Mammuthus primigenius,* which appeared in cave paintings, and the Mastodon, *Mammut sp.* The Ancient Elephant, *Loxodonta antiqua,* is related to the African Elephant, *Loxodonta africana.* The Asian Elephant, *Elephos maximus* is a separate genus from a later development. The evolution of the Elephant can therefore be traced from very basic beginnings but it will be unlikely to evolve any further if it is exterminated for its ivory. The African and Asian Elephants are the only living species of this large family of which fossil remains have been found on every continent. John Saxe's poem describes how '*Six Wise Men of Hindustan*', blind and with no visual ability to 'join the dots', thought the individual parts felt like a wall, or a spear, or a snake, or a tree, or a fan or a rope. Each of them concluded that each piece characterised the whole animal, 'so though each was partly in the right, they were all in the wrong'! There is more to the Elephant than meets the eye?

Artists are quite capable of creating work inspired by Elephants, without involving ivory. They can exploit their vast surface area to accommodate colourful decoration, seen in ceremonial parades in India, a tradition which was brought to the Manchester Day Parade in 2012 when the Indian community of the city demonstrated their techniques on a huge inflatable Elephant, covering its broad flanks with intricate patterns and symbols. A more subtle piece was made by the artist, Bharti Kher from Delhi in the *'Facing East'* exhibition of contemporary sculptures from the Frank Cohen collection shown at Manchester City Art Gallery in 2010. The sculptural form of a life-size Asian Elephant has its skin decorated with patterns of wriggling sperm. He called the piece *'The skin speaks a language not its own'*, but you are left wondering whether the Elephant is no longer of this world or does it have its ear to the ground, listening for a response to that language? This image of an Elephant is not likely to be forgotten.

Bear Market

'Polar' was a cinematic portrait of the ice caps with a live orchestral soundtrack by Manchester Camerata at the RNCM. This genre recreated the old silent movie experience but with coloured images and a richer musical content to respond to the character of the animals and their polar habitat.

I must agree that the Elephant certainly has an undeniable presence, but it is more often seen as a beast of burden rather than a creature to which children can relate on a personal level. The Lion has already pointed out that many animals have been popular muses for painters and sculptors but Bears are not approachable creatures because deep down we are, as a species, really quite shy. It comes from living a lone existence whether that be in Arctic wastes or more temperate forests. That seems to make us unattainable, and somehow more attractive? Associations with Bears take grownups back to their childhood when their closest companion was a Teddy Bear. In their natural habitat, rather than the nursery or even the art gallery, Polar Bears are nothing like that; they can be particularly savage if they have new-born cubs to protect. The artist, Chen Lei, challenges this dichotomy and makes us look again at the value of our relationships in his piece 'The Big Kiss', another work from the Frank Cohen collection in the 'Facing East' exhibition in the City Art Gallery. This explored the close connection between animals and humans in a surreal and precarious balance between a child and a Polar Bear. With the phenomenon of global warming being blamed for the endangered state of the Polar Bear, could this be interpreted as the 'Kiss of Death'? Or perhaps this is simply a piece about developing a deeper trust in relationships so friendships can be more than superficial?

Polar Bears need sea ice on which to live during the winter months but their Arctic habitat is extremely sensitive to climatic changes. Towards the end of the 20th century, sea ice had been reduced by almost a half, both in extent and in thickness, indicating that it is likely to disappear altogether throughout the summer sometime during the 21st century. What we Polar Bears will do then is anybody's guess. We are hardly likely to survive if we migrate south to go native with the other Bears because we would stand out like a sore thumb in their territory. Unless we hibernate during the summer, I don't know how long it would take to evolve into something a little less white so we could develop some sort of camouflage? I don't believe that hunters would allow us that luxury. The displays in the Manchester Museum have been subtly rearranged to set historic specimens from their collections in a more questioning context so they might get everybody to put on their thinking caps and help us to find a solution, or insist that those with power and influence can move in the right direction. Otherwise you will only know about us through exhibits like the stuffed Polar Bear which was obtained as a flat skin from the whaling ship, SS Eclipse. Captain Milne gave it to the Albert Institute and Victoria Galleries in Dundee who passed it on, in 1907, to the Manchester Museum where taxidermist, Harry Brazenor, prepared it and mounted it in its present glory so that even Sir Edwin Landseer would feel safe enough to paint its portrait.

The Manchester Museum Ice Bear

The precarious state of Polar Bears has triggered responses to global warming, extending the animal conservation theme to the environment, presumably in the rather forlorn hope that people are more likely to take the conservation of the planet seriously if their own existence is threatened? This theme has been explored in various artistic and scientific installations, and one political statement on climate change was commissioned by the Manchester Museum to mark the opening of their new Living Worlds Gallery in 2011. Their '*Ice Bear*' was a dynamic 10-tonne block of ice, sculpted into the form of a large Polar Bear by artist Mark Coreth. It was set up in Piccadilly Gardens and allowed to melt, in an exceptional mini heat wave which accelerated the process, to reveal a permanent bronze skeleton of the Bear. Afterwards, the skeleton briefly occupied a site opposite the Museum on Oxford Road to attract attention to the new gallery highlighting particular aspects of human behaviour which impact on the animal and plant communities on which, humans seem to have forgotten, they also depend. By discussing the globalisation of commercial exploitation of natural resources, the effects of war, superstitions and beliefs, along with the aftermath of natural disasters and other influences it must be hoped that it will become possible to devise a programme to balance all these factors. Otherwise, as they say, we're all in this together and there will be no winners if nothing is done. It may already be too late?

Artists have a long tradition of contributing to political debates by challenging people's perceptions and without wishing to blow a trumpet, in case it be mistaken for an Elephant, Bears have featured in their work as much as other animals. The Staffordshire earthenware blue Bear made around 1812, a critical point in European history, gives Napoleon an intimate hug not with any ardent intent but to squeeze the breath out of him before he can achieve his aim to rule the world. Anti-bearbaiting sentiments in the Staffordshire jug from the same period suggest that the Bear intends a similar fate for the Dog? Paul Smith creates a tender hug for an intimate relationship between Goldilocks and an amorous Bear. However, this has a darker side which stands the menacing aspect of the fairy tale on its head. Is it Goldilocks who is giving the hug? The Bear may look rapt and innocent but he is still armed with lethal claws, so he can be trusted only if she can? In the Royal Exchange Craft Shop, more pieces by Paul Smith challenge perceptions of innocence as small Polar Bears, juggling with fish, evoke memories of the nursery or the nature of a kitten with a ball of wool, but he does not let you forget that this Bear is a killing machine which is fighting for survival in its natural habitat.

So imagine finding a pair of Polar Bears outside the Chinese Arts Centre, pushing a huge snowball around the streets of the Northern Quarter as a statement about climate change. Then I thought I heard mention of Dung Beetles with a different conservation message? But they were neither Bears nor Beetles. They were symbolic Sheep! Their snowball was a ball of wool as part of an installation by Chinese performance artists, He Hai and Deng Dafei of the Utopia Group. Their *Enclosure* installation dealt with the appropriation of common land by rich landowners in 16th century Britain which established capitalism as an economic power. The artists followed a closed circular route around the city to symbolise these enclosures, relating this to current Chinese experience by demonstrating that the Sheep, representing people who have been shorn of their resources, still had to work in textile mills and factories. They pushed the ball backwards to indicate how difficult working conditions could destroy people physically and mentally, reflecting the observations of Friedrich Engels on the condition of the working classes in Manchester in the 1840s. Participants in this commercial relay race of production currently import the same agony in the form of cheap fashions, often made in China under worse conditions than those of the 19th century wage slaves in Britain. It just goes to show that first impressions can be very misleading, although the work did produce a variety of reactions and encouraged discussion with the artists: better to be wrong with good intent than to be absolutely unmoved! It is rare for a Bear Market to be created by Sheep even if they were disguised as Polar Bears - or Dung Beetles? Although it suggests that abundant fundamental problems do not seem to be endangered in the same way as Polar Bears.

Look Both Ways

The Agnus Dei, Lamb of God, became a title for Jesus and the figure of the Lamb bearing a cross or flag was the symbol of Christ. This appears in the tympanum above the entrance of St Mary's Church in Mulberry Street, Manchester's 'Hidden Gem', making a connection with the Roman roots of the city.

Sheep grazing on the grassy slopes of defensive ditches outside the Roman fort, established in Castlefield in 79AD, were likely to become animal sacrifices to household gods to bring peace and prosperity to the family, the home and the town. Soothsayers would indulge in divination, poking around in the entrails of the Sheep in search of news, although why they couldn't wait for a man with a message in a cleft stick and get it in writing beats me. Underground messages for Christians in this remote outpost were hidden in a wordsquare tablet found in the archeological excavations around the fort. It was designed to encourage the new religion to take root and is unusual in that it has five layers rather than the more common four layers. It must have been extremely effective because by the time the Roman army was recalled to defend Rome in 406AD, most of Britain was Christian. The obscure messages in the wordsquare amongst the puzzles in the Manchester Evening News maintain this tradition. Near the fort, the sculpture of 'Sheep' made by Ted Roocroft in1986 still attracts underground messages and was decorated with knitted flags of Britain, USA and Israel by 'urban interventionists', Shift//Delete, as a piece of anonymous street art around central narratives of social, environmental and spatial justice issues which sounds like an awful burden for simple Sheep to have to bear? We thought it was a bit ironic that all the symbolism, which went right over our heads, should put the wool back on the Sheep where it belonged - and we're still puzzling over its significance. Or were they trying to pull the wool over our eyes? Somebody must have understood it because it took the prize at the CUBE Open exhibition in 2011. Sheep are not really leaders and are more renowned for following so after getting the Polar Bear 'Enclosures' incident so wrong, it would be inviting trouble for mere Sheep to pronounce on this one?

As if political symbolism weren't bad enough, people find it very difficult to disentangle some of Aesop's misdirection in order to be able to think laterally so they can reassess some of their conceptions of the nature of animals. Everybody will recognise a Wolf in Sheep's clothing as an enemy posing as a friendly familiar figure, someone hiding their wicked intent under a cloak of false kindness. They forget that the shepherd was in the habit of taking an occasional Sheep for his meat ration and the Wolf stood at risk of becoming that night's supper if the plan backfired? So, what do you think might happen if the Sheep were to appear in Wolf's clothing? In the Whitworth Gallery's collection of textiles, there is a significant theatrical piece which blurs the distinction between Sheep and Wolf, Wolf and Sheep, so that you are never quite sure which is menacing and dangerous, which is innocent and safe. Judith Duffey's pair of costumes examines the timelessness of the human condition and demonstrates the ambiguities which occur when these nemeses come face-to-face.

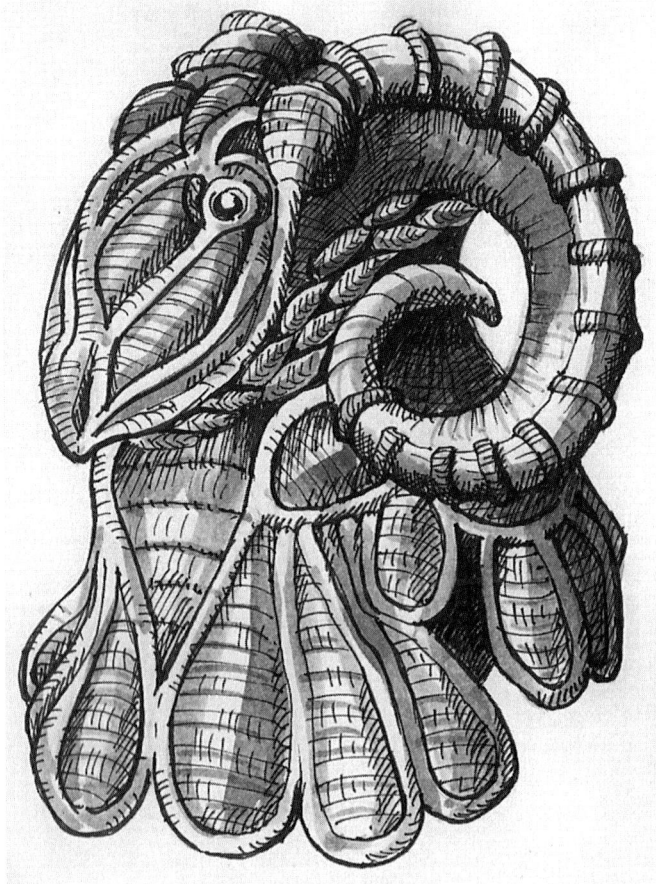

She has created characters which go far beyond the conventions established in the fables to push the work beyond the boundary of a utilitarian domestic craft exercise in knitwear. Never be in any doubt that Wolves are ferocious, cunning, cruel and evil. It is not in the nature of Sheep to take on these characteristics or to abandon their traditional meekness and stupidity, but a Sheep can acquire street credibility and become as dangerous as any Wolf! Do not allow yourself to be mesmerised by the intricacy of the detail. Be aware of the unexpected while you admire the subtle colours, the differences between the hand knitting and the machine techniques which combine variations of stitches and devices like the turning of a sock heel to achieve rugged textures with scale-like overlapping layers, heavy Fair Isle cables, cords and tassels .... This pair of helmet masks and tunics might be made from pure Sheep's wool, but they are not all that they seem. Think twice about the ambivalence in their designs, if you feel you can trust the advice of a Sheep - or a Wolf? Look both ways!

As you get older, you appreciate that fairy tales and fables were nothing more than stories to teach children the concept of morality. It then becomes possible to dream up alternative ways of interpreting things more in sympathy with the animals. We Wolves - or Sheep - are quite capable of indulging in the art of misdirection to create a bit of confusion, make mischief. Take Red Riding Hood. She might well have been nothing like the sweet, innocent, little girl we are supposed to believe she is. How many girls like that do you know? Yes, I expect you are saying that I'm crying 'Wolf', but just look at her a little more closely. 'Game' by Nicola Hicks in her 'Furtive Imagination' exhibition at the Whitworth Art Gallery, challenged the traditional perception of the relationship between the Wolf and a small child. There is no telling which one of them would win the 'game'. She is no longer a vulnerable child, she's a femme fatale, a 21st century young lady. Is she a Sheep in Wolf's clothing? You can't be sure if she's a little girl dressing up to look like she's twenty-something or a young woman dressing in current fashions to look like she's just off to school. What's a real Wolf being encouraged to think? She certainly knows how to turn heads to divert attention from any wickedness she has in mind. What about my wickedness, what am I supposed to do with that? Do I need to adjust my furtive imagination because I don't know any more whether I'm a Wolf or a Sheep? It's all very confusing.

50

Wickedness, furtiveness, deviousness can be bewildering if everybody else is doing it. How do you recognise it under such circumstances? Paul Smith has seen through Red Riding Hood's subterfuge. His ceramic pieces have captured her abstract charm, like a Modigliani painting, with simple forms and subtle colours, distracting your attention from the deeper resonances of a more complex character. He's not afraid to put his head into the Wolf's mouth because he knows that the reward for doing favours will be that he won't lose his head for performing a service, as Aesop's Crane discovered. And if you want to sacrifice a Wolf, would you throw him to the Sheep? The Horse + Bamboo Theatre's interpretation of the fairy tale in the Royal Exchange Studio addressed this ambivalent view when Little Red played bullfighting games with her red cape before beguiling the Wolf with her advances. But the Wolf reverted to type and swallowed her whole. Grandmother had already suffered the same fate, so they escaped by cutting their way out of his stomach with a saw thoughtfully packed by her mother in Red Riding Hood's basket which she had held onto. After this traumatic experience, they worked magic to fly away in the basket tethered beneath a red balloon, leaving the poor Wolf somewhat deflated. It's not easy being a Wolf.

That Red Riding Hood seems to have made a lot of people very cynical because they can no longer take fairy tales at face value for pure enjoyment like they did when they were children. You know very well that Aesop's anthropomorphism wasn't only intended for children. Children aren't stupid. They know that animals can't talk, but they are able to suspend their disbelief whereas grownups have lost that ability and take things more literally. It makes it so complicated for a Wolf to know how to deal with children who become as astute as grownups. Does it really take a talking Wolf - or even a talking Sheep - to point out that human beings have weaknesses that they would prefer not to acknowledge? They know that Aesop was imposing human characteristics on the animals, but they prefer to believe that he was using the animals' weaknesses to make his point. In the same tradition, Charles Perrault's story of Red Riding Hood, in his *History of Tales of Past Times*, inspired composer Jessica Hall at the RNCM to explore the link between music and film. In the spirit of Prokofiev's *Peter and the Wolf*, the characters were assigned different instruments to represent them and the musicians of the Talisma Ensemble were playing in costume to make visual links with the narrative. It felt a little uncomfortable, as the Wolf, to be sitting quite so close to the Woodcutter with a large axe wedged into his French horn, diverting attention from Red Riding Hood and her Grandmother. With all this uncertainty, I begin to fear for the morals of a society that seems to be turning into a pack of Wolves. Perhaps that is why there was a Roman Centurion in the Manchester Day Parade leading his Irish Wolfhound mascot? I must be more careful.

Sheep, with their Lambs, were quite safe in the windows of Jigsaw but they ventured out onto the pavement in Exchange Square for their 'Wool Week' campaign. The resin models were very popular with children, who loved having their photographs taken with them. This distracted the security shepherd who should have been watching his flock by day, and one of the Lambs was rustled from right under his nose. Some poor Wolf will get the blame as the Lamb was last seen being taken towards Victoria Station. If they caught a train to head for the hills, the Lamb could always take refuge in one of the dry stone-walled pens like the reconstruction in the Portland Basin Museum housing a model Ram. Better that than to finish up in the Smithfield Market. The old buildings in the Northern Quarter have been decorated with silhouettes of Sheep and their shepherd cut from Astroturf - not only as a kindness to Sheep but no grass was harmed in this installation! Obviously nothing to do with Wolves; we're not exactly model citizens.

Sleeping Dogs

Dogs in Manchester are a bit like children in the city: they generally are not residents and come for a day out with their owners or to enjoy splashing around in the fountains in Piccadilly Gardens. But there are homeless people on the streets whose only comfort is the company of a faithful Dog.

Some people look upon Dogs as domesticated Wolves because they have no idea what Dogs can do for them. They need to think about Stephen Charock's *People Power*, commissioned by the People's History Museum to welcome visitors to their new extension. The rusted steel sculpture includes figures representing everyone who has fought for the vote, fought for equality and against injustice, all who have given people the freedom they have now and those who are still fighting for the freedom they have not yet achieved. To this they might add the need to make sure that everything which has been achieved so far is properly defended against avaricious corporations who seem to have the power to manipulate our political masters. So they need a good Dog who will bark to make them aware of what's going on. There is a Dog at the head of this gathering of fighters, a Watchdog, ready to be let off his lead in defence of freedom if it is being threatened by the system. Some people have given up the fight because they cannot cope with the demands it makes to give them 'Freedom'. All they get is 'Democracy' which makes no difference to their condition, so they've defined freedom in their own terms and put themselves outside the system. They're more content to live on the streets with a Dog that demands nothing in return. Many people are joining their ranks for one reason or another because those in charge of the system cannot be trusted. The Watchdog is barking and it's time to let him off his lead.

Flat-dwellers in the city centre generally have no pets, so the Northern Quarter has lost its pet shops, clustered in Tib Street like an oriental bazaar. To compensate for the lack of live animals, graffiti artists have created a whole pack of Dogs which briefly decorate walls and shutters to add colour to the defences of businesses. Guard Dogs, you might call them, appear in a bewildering variety of techniques, ranging from the ubiquitous spray paints to sophisticated stencilled forms, poster style collages glued to signposts, street furniture and switch boxes. The new tile mosaic on the Black Dog Ballroom began the revival of the artwork around Affleck's Palace and is an incarnation of the neon logo above their door. Koffee Pot café's Dog's have lost their friends on the walls and bar shutters in Stevenson Square. In the nature of graffiti, Dogs disappear but others pop up to celebrate success elsewhere. You can't keep a good Dog down.

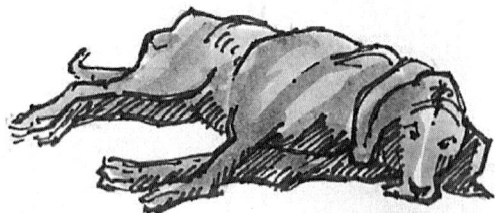

Ephemeral portraits in the Urban Jungle contrast with those in the paintings in the collection of the City Art Gallery. The relationship between a boy and his Dog, explored in Briton Riviere's 1871 painting of '*My only friend*', has Dickensian echoes of the exploitation of child labour which was well documented by Friedrich Engels in Manchester. Children, escaping from the grim conditions in mills, would abandon their families to take their chances in the outside world which generally served only to increase the numbers of vagrants. Their situation mirrors that of the homeless people who currently live rough on the city streets and a Dog would certainly have been the only friend of such children. Dogs don't abandon their people or their duties, as demonstrated in Riviere's 1875 picture, '*Last of the garrison*', a romantic view of a Royalist Bloodhound who stayed to defend the manor house, dying in the doorway where the woodwork has been blasted by a cannonball and all the human defendants have disappeared. I feel flattered by the pictures but I've noticed that nothing pleases people more than a good model, particularly small models which make them feel like Gulliver in Lilliput. Cardboard figures of Retrievers were developed as kits by Liam Hopkins and Richard Sweeney for Lazerian in both small and life-size. Their model was their mascot, '*Gerald*', who has become an international celebrity and has enjoyed a reunion with his friends in New York but hasn't forgotten his roots. The magic of these figures in geometric shapes is that they have managed to convey the animated spirit of the Dogs better than any of the paintings or the graffiti. But, in the city, we Dogs are a still a minority group, a bit like Horses in a mechanised world.

Horse Power

If Adolphe Valette had been present to witness the Police Mounted Division confronting students in Albert Square, he might have recorded one of their demonstrations against changes to the financing of higher education in one of his impressionist paintings. He had been a tutor at the Manchester School of Art, outside which he took an artist's interest in horse-drawn vehicles.

When I turned up, there were already lots of patients waiting to have their feet attended to, along with other unmentionable conditions. They were prepared to divulge little bits of gossip to avoid having to disclose their personal details. Must keep some things private. It didn't take long for us all to agree that, as a minority group, our interests weren't being taken seriously. Motorists create the biggest problems, always shouting the loudest: not enough parking, charges too excessive, pedestrians jaywalking, one way streets all point the wrong way. They must have got lost in the Northern Quarter? As there was no movement in the queue, the conversation turned to families. Not wishing to boast, it was easier to score points if there was a celebrity tethered under the family tree. It was debatable as to what constituted a celebrity but some had family connections in Chinatown where they seem to have a different outlook. They used to treat their ancestors like gods and put models in their graves, a bit like the Pharaohs in ancient Egypt. It was important that they should have household goods, musical instruments, servants to wait on them in the afterlife and, of course, their faithful steed had pride of place as a fine piece of ceramic like those in the City Art Gallery. Horses were treated like gods themselves, as figures on the roof tiles protecting houses, shown in the 'China' exhibition at the Manchester Museum. Those days of applied symbolism have gone as Horses don't play such an important part in people's lives any more. Certainly all those patients waiting for attention didn't feel the least bit godly.

As in all walks of life, some of us have things easier than those who have to work hard for their living, like Pack Horses, somebody said. Their family had been in the transport industry when Pack Horses struggled on unmade roads left by the Romans and hardly mended for over a thousand years. Then some bright engineer designed roads that made it possible to use vehicles with wheels and, of course, it was Horses who provided the power to drive them: cabs, carriages, wagons, even trams. For everyday getting about in the city there was the Hansom cab with the driver perched high at the back, or coach with the driver at the front. Adolphe Valette, who taught at the Manchester School of Art, painted the Horses in All Saints and Albert Square in his atmospheric paintings which hang in the City Art Gallery. The carriages rattling over the granite cobbles would shake up the passengers a bit, but the Horses got a change of scenery and a few breaks between fares. The poor work Horses who walked around in circles all day, winding the lifting gear for a coal mine, like the reconstruction in the Museum of Science and Industry, would send miners down, haul up one tub of coal after another, and then incur the wrath of the mine-owners if they got tired and had to stop. What about the poor Horses? The owners were too mean to get a second pair even if they could get better production from a couple working in relays. And, because pit ponies were out of sight underground, they were also out of mind as they hauled heavy loads from the coalface to the lift shaft. Some work Horses enjoyed fresh country air and variable English weather as they pulled carts and farm machinery or did ploughing. But when the military started their Great War in 1914, they requisitioned these trained Horses to do similar work under more hostile conditions - and under enemy fire. This was the inspiration for Michael Morpurgo's book 'War Horse' which was made into a play and a film.

The Imperial War Museum North exhibition, '*Once Upon a Wartime*', illustrating the background of stories for children about war experiences, included a wooden Horse used to train soldiers to equip a Horse with saddle, harness, reins, bridle and stirrups before they were let loose on live animals which reacted in a way that lifeless wooden models could not prepare them for! Individual Mules carried boxes of ammunition while teams of Mules pulled carts of equipment and heavy guns up to the front lines, up to their fetlocks in Flanders mud as the only means of moving stuff in that swamp. The military depended on Horses, but when rations got scarce, soldiers weren't averse to eating them. Better that, they reckoned, than having to retreat and let the other side eat them. They had no idea how many animals they had in the battlefield and guessed that it was probably between one and two million, but a quarter of them died on active duty.

To herald the arrival of *'War Horse'* at the Lowry Theatre and to mark the Anniversary of the start of the First World War in 2014, the Portland Basin Museum commissioned artist Juliette Hamilton to create a life-size model of 'Joey' in woven willow. She used dark canes, some stripped to make the white blaze on his forehead and the white socks round his ankles and, because the willow itself has life in it, the finished sculpture is very much alive. The stage production of the play used life-sized sophisticated puppets animated by skilled operators to represent the animals. The film based on Michael Morpurgo's book changed the original text to suit the cinematic aspirations of the director but it still managed to show the full horror of the universal suffering of the combatants, the local people who found themselves living in the middle of the battlefield and the animals caught up in it, none of whom were in a position to make judgements on those who had shattered everybody's world. That was supposed to be the 'War to end all War', so what did they do next? They didn't abandon war because, paradoxically, they had become accustomed to that as a means of conflict resolution, so they didn't bother to look for a humane alternative. They pensioned off the cavalry and invented more sophisticated weapons. What they call 'escalation' which meant higher profits for arms dealers who therefore have a vested interest in starting wars while politicians try to pretend they're just maintaining a balance of power. They play their war games on computers instead of maps with model soldiers, but they still put real people and animals into the battlefield. It seems that 'Horse sense' is a commodity that won't let them make a profit?

In the Great War the officers rode on Horseback into the face of new technology which included machine guns to mow them down like the fields of corn they flattened with their Hounds in pursuit of a Fox. They believed they were still living in a medieval world of chivalry with its moral, social and religious code, but knighted Generals no longer led the charge. They commanded the battle from a safe distance to suit the conditions of modern warfare. It was all very well for a Knight to put his life in the hands of God while he was cased in armour which added to the load his faithful Horse had to carry. The poor Horse had no idea what to expect when he took the Knight on a quest, faced with going into the darkest cave to overcome evil. If Knights hadn't a clue what was lurking in the depths of the darkness, it was hardly surprising that it frightened the Horses - and the Hounds. Such apprehension was captured by Briton Riviere in his painting '*In Manus Tuas Domine*' in 1879. He dreamed up images for these romantic tales of medieval Knights who went to fight evil so they could come back and tell awe-inspiring stories of how brave they had been, killing dragons and things. But they never brought back any 'evidence' to prove what they had done. I mean, you didn't need them to drag a whole carcass of a dragon behind them, but had anyone ever seen so much as half a yard of dragon's tail or a dragon's ear or a tooth or a toe nail? Of course not! I reckon they made it all up and relied on the Horse not to expose their fairy tales of bravery.

Now if it's bravery you want, you couldn't do better than the Roman chariot races, with a charioteer perched in a little cart, bouncing along behind four great Horses going at full tilt round the Hippodrome with the crowds cheering them on. Just look at Alexander von Wagner's painting of the 'Chariot Race' in the City Art gallery. That's what I call bravery. And, you will note, that they named the stadium after the Horses, not the men in the chariots, so they got their priorities right. If a chariot lost a wheel, that would be the end of the charioteer; if he didn't break his neck when he hit the ground, he'd be squashed under the next chariot. I suppose that made the act more like stupidity than bravery? In two thousand years they haven't learned much. They still race Horses over fences, over ditches, whipping them to go faster for 'sport'. Then they chase defenceless animals across the landscape, with or without fences, when all the Horse wants is a nice field with good grazing. If the Horse feels he needs a bit of exercise he can always gallop around a bit, but there's never a protester to shout about animal rights when you really need one. The Empire-builders from Europe went to practise their horsemanship in their colonies in the New World and virtually wiped out the North American Indians along with their buffalo herds. They rounded up the few remaining specimens of the Indians, because that's how they saw them, to put in 'Wild West Shows'. Buffalo Bill brought his show to Belle Vue in 1887 but the Indians were more interested in a ride on the tram, saving their bareback riding, acrobatics and stunts for the show which was something like a circus - another invention of the Romans!

But it wasn't just the people in the colonies who suffered. The Authorities did some very uncivilised things to the poor devils who didn't manage to escape from the Peterloo massacre in 1819. Some were lucky and found refuge with the Quakers in Mount Street after demonstrating for their democratic rights for proper political representation. However, the magistrates misread the situation and, in a panic, ordered the cavalry to clear Peter's Field. The cavalrymen had been drinking and should never have been sent in to do a sensitive job in that state. They said they were only following orders, but did they have to be so brutal? And it's not so far back in our democratic history that it gives politicians a right to criticise foreign governments for doing the same thing today. We're on the other side of the fence now so they should learn from our experience, not repeat it. For some years, there's been a campaign to commemorate the events of Peterloo with a monument, but what might be the first equestrian statue in the city will need to be designed to make sure that it doesn't glorify the horsemen but respects the 18 people who lost their lives, along with 654 injured? The Unions haven't forgotten what happened at Peterloo. They know that unity is strength and the politicians are trying to chip away the rights that were won all those years ago. The Manchester RMT Union have incorporated the message in their banner, designed and made by Ed Hall and displayed in the exhibition 'On the March' at the People's History Museum.

Reproduced by kind permission of Ed Hall

The Romans would have loved the mechanical Horses on the Carousel that comes to Manchester at Christmas. I know it's really for children, but grownups enjoy it as well, so they still have their instinct to gallop about the world. Those Horses going round and round, and up and down, make me jealous with all their bright colours and gold ornament - like the bling on royal carriages. And the music makes me want to dance. The only other Horses left in the city are Police Horses. When you see them ready to charge crowds of rioters, you wonder which side of the fence they're on - not that they have to jump over fences, of course. That Snodgrass thinks it's a grand day out for him to chase protestors. He's not been the same since he was chosen to be a model for Korean sculptor, Gwon Osang, for his exhibition 'Deodorant Type' at the City Art Gallery. I can see why they picked him. He's a handsome fellow, but the celebrity seems to have gone to his head. I do believe he thinks he's some sort of film star, like from a wild west movie except he can't find any red Indians to persecute. So he'll just have to make the most of students for the moment - unless we have any more riots? He loves to get polished up for a grand parade with his rider wearing a ceremonial helmet with a white horsehair plume. Talk about a big head - Snodgrass, not the rider. That outsize broom and shovel in Thomas Street was made for his outsize droppings.

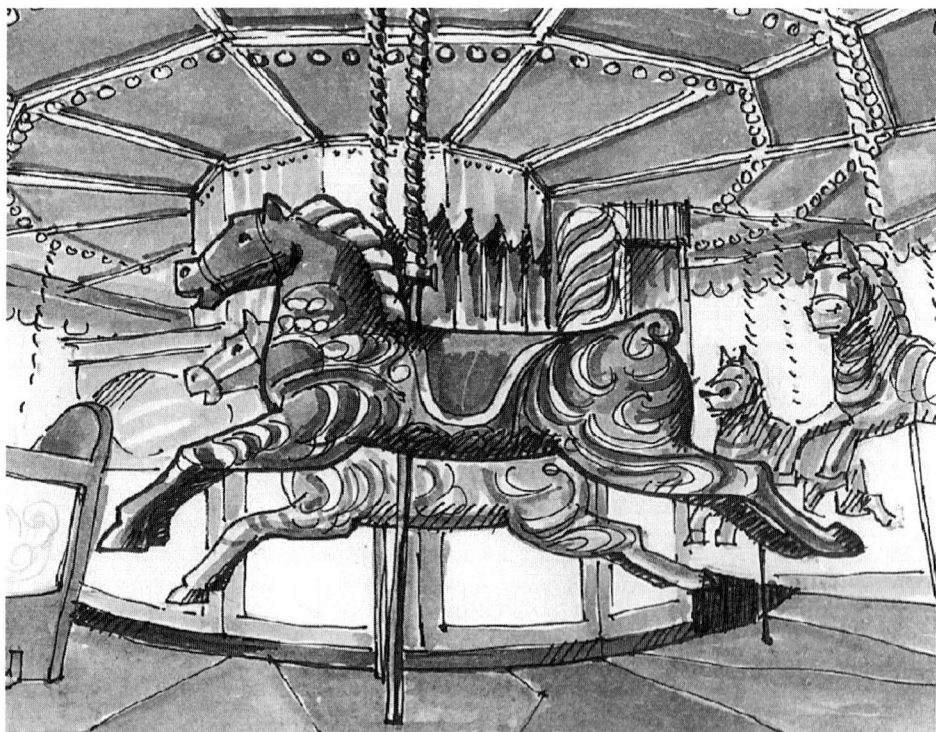

Ah, the farrier will see me now? I thought he was having his picture painted like that one in the City Art Gallery by George Morland in 1793. He would take a different view of life in the city today. His ideas of rural life in the 18th century weren't half as romantic as he would have you believe. It was a case of one rule for the rich who could ride on a Horse and another for the poor who had to walk everywhere. That's how they came to amass lots of private wealth and generate even more public squalor. So when you look around today, you'll see that things haven't changed much. You can take that straight from the Horse's mouth.

Monkey Business

'Monkey' by Andrew Gilmour looks back at the viewer, not accusingly but questioningly, asking if you are going to leave him on the wall of the Cornerhouse, or will you have the courage to take him home? I took him home, not for animal testing but for company. He's well trained.

If those Horses spent less time gossiping, they might find the time to do something a bit more creative. Now, it's no coincidence that philosophers, or was it linguists or mathematicians, believed that if you could train an infinite number of Monkeys to use typewriters - or even word processors in these days of modern technology - sooner or later they would reproduce the works of Shakespeare? Monkeys are smarter than that! We already have the works of Shakespeare, so would they not be more inclined to produce something original? They are very imaginative animals so they might even create something which would transcend the contribution of the Bard? Then, we would have to ask, is there anyone who would recognise a work of genius produced under such circumstances? In order to arrive at that situation, we must first arrange for the Monkeys to be given appropriate training. Those in the Blank Space Gallery look hardly house-trained and Andrew Gilmour's friends at the Cornerhouse look much too laid back, so a trip to Piccadilly Station would seem to be a good place to start because that is where you will find an infinite number of trains. There is also a constant stream of broadcast instructions to make sure that all who enter its teeming concourse get properly trained.

> 'Due to today's wet weather, please take particular care whilst in the station as surfaces may be slippery'.

They have already noticed that we have amongst us some devious characters who will slip imperceptibly into a subversive state as they enrol on the programme.

> 'Please take care when using the escalators. Passengers with perambulators and cycles should use the lifts'.

Monkeys understand that young parents don't use perambulators any more. They have monstrous buggies, infernal machines which must have come with instructions on how to fold them but neither parent has a degree in engineering.

Monkeys, being obedient law-abiding creatures, will have heeded the notices informing them that the riding of cycles is not permitted in the station. The same goes for skateboards and roller-blades but, apparently, monstrous buggies are permitted. But we must get down to the business of producing a work of genius.

'Please do not leave luggage unattended'.

So the Monkeys must not reserve a seat with an unattended typewriter while they go to buy a cup of tea. Don't the authorities know that, if you buy a sticky bun with your tea, it takes two hands to carry your purchases so you must leave your typewriter unattended until the errand has been completed? We are here to learn creative writing not to practise juggling hot liquids, sticky buns and typewriters. So forget the sticky bun and take a healthy piece of fruit. Fruit must be good for the brain because people can't manage without a Blackberry, or an Apple, or an Orange, and now they can teach children computer programming with a credit card-sized gadget called a Raspberry Pie? Nobody seems to have considered that Monkeys might prefer the pie or a simple Banana? Perhaps they had difficulties with Banana skins which may be slippery in today's wet weather? Or should we apply for a course at the 'Ape and Apple'?

'Unattended luggage may be removed or destroyed by Security Services'.
Philistines are patrolling the station, intent on nipping creativity in the bud by annihilating innocent unattended typewriters and fruit salads.

'Secure luggage facilities are located on Platform 10 to enable passengers to store their luggage'.

Unless the secure facility is a prison, a typewriter can't be used unless the Monkey can be stored with it. The Monkey can't be a passenger until it gets on a train. It can't get on a train without its typewriter which is incarcerated in a secure facility.

The Pub/Zoo

MATT & PHREDS

We are having problems with definitions which seek to impose a 'one-size-fits-all' solution on a problem not of our making. If the Monkey is hungry because he has been denied a sticky bun and he has been obliged to put his typewriter in a storage facility which conflicts with his status as a passenger, the argument moves in a circle. A vicious circle! Life is complicated enough without all these meaningless rules and regulations. And we haven't yet considered the impact of a Banana.

> *'Manchester Piccadilly is a no smoking station. Please refrain from smoking whilst at this station'.*

This is what happens when you switch from steam trains to diesels. Heaven help us when it all goes electric with no polluting fumes at all. But what is a Monkey to do to calm his nerves when he has withdrawal symptoms from being denied the pleasures of sticky buns and has been estranged from his beloved typewriter?

> *'Security personnel tour this station 24 hours a day'.*

So no chance for a Monkey to sneak a quiet fag while nobody is looking.

> *'All Monkey Business will be frowned upon and any infringement of the regulations will be dealt with most severely'.*

Is that part of the training? There must be a lot of people who missed the connection for that particular module of the course. Don't these people know that writers need stimulation from nicotine, caffeine, alcohol or other interesting substances? Monkeys are already on this downward slope to creativity as their image has acquired some sort of connection with the intake of alcohol. The 'Pub/Zoo' sign in Grosvenor Street even shows a Monkey with a glass in his hand. Have they been over-indulging in Happy Hour at Matt and Phred's with cool jazz? Works of pure genius would never have seen the light of day if the writer had not been under the influence of one thing or another.

'Due to the late arrival of connecting services, Transpennine Express apologise for the delayed departure of the 12.20 to Cleethorpes'.

The prospect of a trip to Cleethorpes doesn't exactly stir the creative juices so let us hope that this is not the train we need to connect our keyboard skills with our communication techniques in our quest to produce a work of eternal value.

'This is a platform alteration: the 12.30 to Manchester Airport will now leave from Platform 8'.

Now, there's an offer that will be very hard to refuse. What more could a Monkey seeking information hope for? Up, up and away, with or without a typewriter, to a place where the sun shines and says 'welcome home' to a place where you can smoke, drink, leave luggage anywhere you like and perhaps indulge in a spot of skateboarding - or better still, surfboarding - and a never-ending supply of Bananas and Mangos and Papayas. Forget Apples and Oranges and Blackberries and Raspberry Pies - and even the cream. Just make sure that there is a ready supply of ice.

'Please travel in the front train only'.

Excuse me? These instructions are becoming deeply philosophical. Even the smartest Monkey can only travel in one train at a time. If there is only one train, do we watch this space in case another train arrives or do we watch the one train disappear because there was nothing in front? Will the lonely train remain the front train or will another train arrive and make it no longer the front train? What happens if a long train comes into the platform to be divided into two sections because there has been a problem with the rolling stock? Then the first half becomes the front train but the other half, which had been part of the front train, will again become the front train if the first half departs? If this also requires a platform alteration, life begins to get extremely complicated. There is also the possibility that two trains could be joined together but passengers will only recognise the front half because they fear that the rear half may somehow dematerialise before it reaches its destination and therefore travels empty in order to preserve the integrity of the front train? There is a dichotomy concerning the resolution of time and space which the best-trained Monkey would need to debate with brains of a higher order than Einstein. It might even be necessary to arrange a significant intake of alcohol to lubricate the brain cells and a dense cloud of tobacco smoke to obscure all irrelevant distractions. The philosophy of railway operators confirms their scientific affinity with trained Monkeys revealed by the analysis of DNA which indicates that we share many common genes with other members of the animal kingdom - and with plants! If the dear departed Queen Victoria thought that Orangutans were 'frightfully and painfully and disagreeably human', how would she have felt if she had known that she was related to a turnip - a majestic vegetable from one of the Royal Estates, of course?

72

Monkeys would not be the least surprised; they only wish to be given the recognition they deserve. No more use of derogatory terms like Grease Monkeys who are really skilled motor mechanics from another branch of the primate family tree. The 'Old Monkey' in Portland Street has retired from distinguished service delivering explosives and ammunition to Lord Nelson's gunners on the 'Victory'. He survived that better than being press-ganged as a child soldier for modern warfare in Africa in Amanda Dalton's production of 'Powder Monkey' at the Royal Exchange Studio. Now he has opted for the quiet life and taken employment in partnership with an organ-grinder.

> 'The 12.40 to Blackpool Gateau will call at Manchester tart, Oxford roux, Salford croissant and Chorley cake. Please make your selection from the front tray only. Do not leave your porridge unattended or it will be destroyed or devoured by the Security personnel who eat at this station 24 hours a day'.

Is there a problem with the predictive text programme or has a 'Word Monkey' been given an exercise as work experience on the public address system? In a brave attempt to deliver a deep and meaningful message, his labours on the typewriter have either revealed a craving for patisseries or he's made a few typographical errors? Perhaps this is as close as we can expect to come to pure genius, unless the Monkey has aspirations to convert his craving for ornamental pastries into a career in architecture instead? Or perhaps he should apply for a job as a copywriter with Banksy who seems to be the only one who really knows what we're training for. NOISE Festival's exhibition, 'The Art of Protest' at the Peoples History Museum, says it all with his message for the future? The Monkeys really are going to take over the world - if we can get on the write train?

Herd Instinct

Mrs Gaskell and her family moved out of Manchester to rent the house at 84 Plymouth Grove in a rural suburb with views across adjacent fields. The house was built in 1838 and has since been absorbed into the urban village of Longsight.

Elizabeth Gaskell could have taught the Monkeys a thing or two about writing, but she was occupied by thoughts of other animals. The house in Plymouth Grove was ideally suited to her family because it gave them the opportunity to rent pasture in the field across the road for a Cow, like me, so that they could make their own butter. They kept less prestigious ducks, chickens and a pig in the yard behind the house. Mrs Gaskell relaxed in this rural retreat where it was private enough to allow her to be seen outside without her bonnet. What would she have thought about today's fashions? It's not just bonnets that young ladies don't wear. Sometimes I wonder if they got dressed in the dark with their underwear on top of their day clothes? Mrs G would have been mortified! However, her admiration of the Cow probably fired an interest in domestic articles which celebrated our amenable nature. She would have appreciated the 18th century Staffordshire earthenware creamers and might have aspired to owning a silver piece with chased decoration, made in London in 1762, all in the Craft and Design collection in the City Art Gallery along with many similar artefacts. Around this time, we Cows had become an emblem of an idyllic existence in the countryside for a movement of Romantics who were content to admire this from a distance, detaching themselves from the reality of the lives of the rustic peasants on whom the shape of that landscape depended. Those dilettante artists had never experienced the demanding toil carried out by rural workers whose situation was anything but romantic, so Mrs Gaskell probably managed to enjoy her Cow with a little help from her friends - and a servant or two to apply the silver polish to her trinkets?

The sustaining nature of the Cow promoted our elevation to the status of a religious icon and the 'Sacred Cows' of Hindu custom have entered the language in a broader context. I'm sure there have always been iconic institutions in the city which considered themselves to be immune from criticism, reconstruction or complete demolition and they have survived by raising diversionary issues to maintain their cult status. Many organisations around Manchester were keen to be involved in the 'Cow Parade' event in 2004 when 150 life-size resin models of Cows in standing, grazing and resting poses, were decorated to reflect links between the artists and their communities in the selection of details to be applied to the models. At last, someone recognised that Cows are not threatening creatures, in spite of our size, although this became an advantage in providing broad areas on which artists could exercise their imagination. Such a bold gesture was a little ironic in Manchester where collaborations of this kind are second nature to creative people, so their inventive designs generated some truly awful puns.

Cows which graced city streets, open spaces, and the interiors of some buildings, were eventually auctioned to raise funds for local charities. In their new homes, some welcome visitors in office foyers, some were put out to grass on lawns between Urban Splash's Castlefield apartment blocks. 'Manchester Moonflection', originally located in New Cathedral Street and sponsored by Marketing Manchester, the city's tourist office, now resides in the temporary offices of the City Council at Number One First Street. The designers intended that observers should see their own reflection in the mirrored surface of the Cow and become part of the image with its map highlighting features of the city. In its new location, not only do they become part of the installation but they can also see their reflection alongside that of the city's most prominent feature, the Beetham Tower, in the window in front of the Cow. This adds another chapter in the history of the city which was illustrated by Ford Maddox Brown in his murals in the Great Hall of the Town Hall, one of which shows the scientist, John Dalton, collecting marsh-fire gas whilst children observe what they must have thought was an eccentric old man playing in their pond. The brown Cow looking over the fence appears to have more curiosity than the children, but Cows are like that. They don't want to miss anything!

When they're not looking over fences to watch the world go by, Cows might spend their days chewing the cud. Their rumination demonstrates a more contemplative, darker side which was exploited by Nicola Hicks in her exhibition of 'Furtive Imagination' at the Whitworth Art Gallery in 1996. The installation 'Fee, Fie, Foe, Fum' was a herd of Cows intimidating enough to chill the blood of any Englishman who might stand in their way. The fabrication of the beasts from straw and mud-like plaster, represents the elements of their natural habitat, somehow making them more like living animals than the mass-produced resin models of Cow Parade. You can't beat the hand-crafted animation created by the vigorous texture which gave these creatures a significant presence without depending on quirky visual puns. Jack the Giant-killer had sold his mother's Cow for a bag of magic beans, so these Cows were out for revenge!

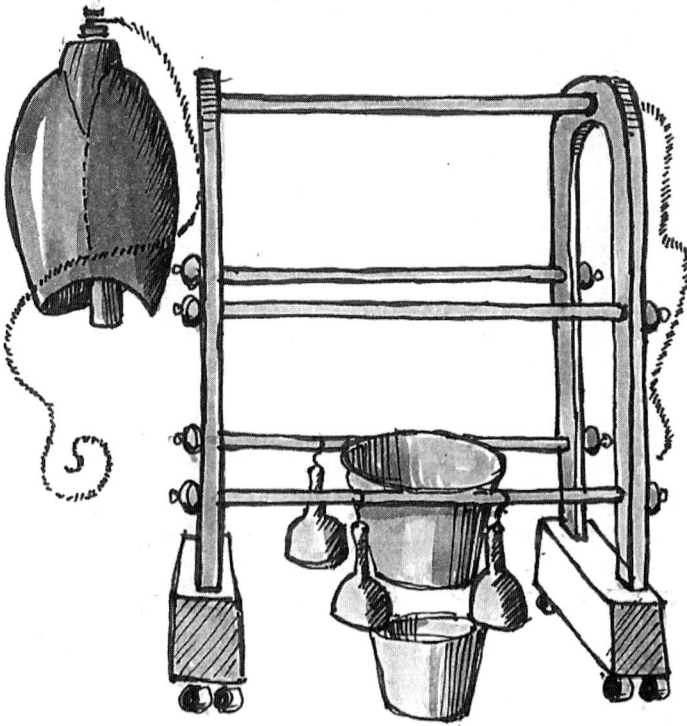

However, it would appear that we Cows are paradoxical animals in that we can represent maternal nourishment without endearing ourselves to children because of our overwhelming size. Children can be very surprised when they encounter a real cow for the first time, one that breathes and moves and smells. In the pantheon of their soft toys, more threatening species like Bears have been accepted because they walk upright on occasions, like the children who relate to them, especially if a little anthropomorphism is applied to cement the bond. Cows, on our four legs, are not blessed with cuddly fur or intimate soft contours - and a pair of horns doesn't help. I suppose that we must be satisfied that we have been able to succeed as pantomime figures which exploit our nurturing characteristics as a foil to the wickedness of the villain - who, on occasions, has also been blessed with demonic horns and a tail. I'm not so sure about the 'stripped down' caricature constructed by the RNCM in their production of Stephen Sondheim's fantasia on nursery rhymes, 'Into the Woods'. They presented the Cow as an assembly of its essential characteristics - complete with a large cowbell because the designer was a musician. This is all very well as an abstract composition, but to apply the elements to .... a Clotheshorse? What an indignity!

People no longer have Mrs Gaskell's option to keep their own Cow in their back yard for making their own dairy produce as an apocalyptic spectre would descend upon them like a herd of banshees in the form of the Sacred Cow of the Health and Safety Regulations, and no doubt lots more of that ilk. As children become more estranged from the origin of their food and believe that milk only exists in plastic bottles on supermarket shelves, two-dimensional images of Cows are as close as most of them will come to a real Cow. Delivery lorries, which service the stores on Whitworth Street, are disguised in black and white camouflage, hoping that people will make the connection with herds of the same persuasion which produce the milk for Robert Wiseman's Dairies? This presupposes that people have this black and white pattern stored in their memory banks although it is more striking than the plain brown shades of Channel Island breeds, even if the milk doesn't have the same cult status. But this could leave children even more confused if they are diverted from bottles on the shelves to believe that milk is produced by black-and-white lorries? And when they see small lorries in the same livery, will those children believe that the Cow has carelessly allowed its Calf to stray and it is driving around the city in search of its mother? Where will this confusion end?

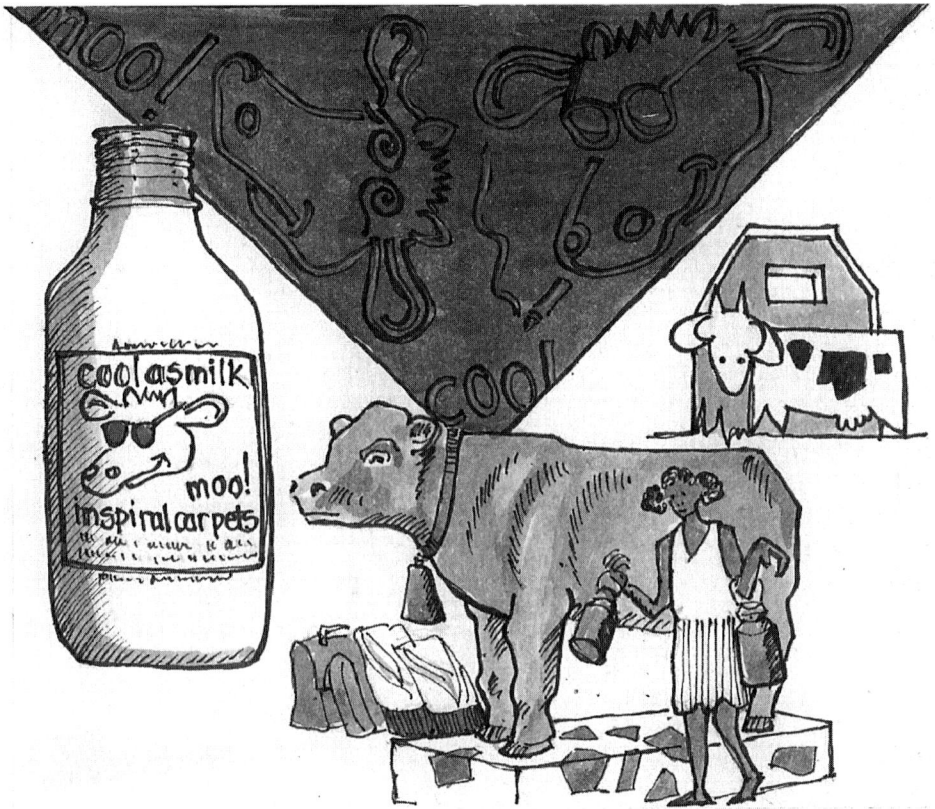

Cows have had several minutes of fame in the illustrious creative atmosphere of Manchester, even in one of the 'different' campaigns by Harvey Nichols who installed a giant Cow in their handbag display. The Cow might have been a little disturbed if it had been aware of any surreal - or practical - connections with leather goods? A small black and white Cow managed to slip in amongst Andrew Gilmour's Monkeys at the Cornerhouse, but many years before that, there had been occasional appearances of Cows in the most unlikely cultural contexts when bands like The Smiths used a soundtrack backing of Cows on their 1985 album, 'Meat is Murder'. At around the same time, Inspiral Carpets decided that milk was 'Cool' and featured cartoon Cow caricatures decorating the labels of milk bottles on their record sleeves. At least they made the connection between milk and cows and this has been immortalised in the cast iron panels set in the pavement of Oldham Street, maintaining links with other bands and venues at which they played around 'Madchester' in the 1980s. It must be hoped that these metallic icons are of sufficient substance to endure until the Cows come home?

We are what we eat

The tragic last act of Bizet's grand opera, 'Carmen',
produced in 2010 by the RNCM, included the colourful
parade of the Banderilleros, the Picadors and the Matador
who delivers the fatal blow to the unfortunate bull offstage
as the death of Carmen is happening in view of the
audience to the background roars of the crowd.

A Bull rearing up, ready to charge, conjured up a connection with the Bullring, especially above the name of 'Torore'. As there was no Bullring in Portland Street, you may have had to suspend your disbelief to imagine the gallant Bull, having lost his battle with Carmen's Matador, Escamillo, being served as steaks for the evening meal as it was always intended he should. Language is no more reliable as a guide than the visual image, as the restaurant served Mexican cuisine with steaks of Argentinian beef, so it should not be forgotten that Spanish culture was spread into Latin America by the 16th century Conquistadors through Venezuela, Mexico and Peru. The last British Bullfighter, Frank 'el Inglés' Evans from Salford, engaged in Bullfighting in Spain and in Latin America, and he advised the RNCM on costume, weapons and showmanship for their production of the grand opera. Bullfighting has links with ancient Rome as a 'warm up' act for gladiatorial contests, but its roots are recorded in prehistoric cave paintings in Spain, suggesting Bull worship and sacrifice. Other restaurants honour the medieval conventions of their signs more faithfully and Nando's chicken shown on their logo will certainly finish up on your plate. It even has its own story written on the wall inside the restaurant to justify its place on the menu. Their finger-food is somewhat conservative compared with the more ostentatious display produced in the kitchens of Ordsall Hall, where an image of what was in the pie was mounted on the crust, preparing the digestive juices for Peacock in a reconstruction of a Tudor delicacy.

So what would you expect from a café displaying an Aardvark as its logo? A search in the 'Oxford Companion to Food' describes this South African anteater as 'one of a kind' and named by Dutch colonists as an 'earth pig' because it digs tunnels in which it lives. Surprisingly, it has a good reputation as food and tastes like pork but it was not on the menu in the café embedded in Blackwell's Bookshop on Oxford Road. However, there was a reason for the logo: the café needed a new name and the owners, looking for a literary connection, found that the first noun in the dictionary was Aardvark, an animal with a distinctive profile. The café has taken Holy Orders and moved across to St Peter's Church, having taught us not to take everything we read at face value as there may be another interpretation. Certainly one would hope that the menu at Chiquito's would not include recipes containing Gecko which decorated the screen outside? And the Donkey logo of Bar Burrito looks far too happy to suggest that he might turn up in a wrap?

BULLS HEAD

THE OX

THIRSTY SCHOLAR

BLUE PARROT

The sign of a Bull or an Ox outside a tavern would certainly not guarantee that beef would be served along with your drink, although with the advent of the gastro-pub, it may be more likely, whereas Unicorn would certainly not be available in Church Street. Artists have been challenged to exercise their imagination to enhance or exploit the more bizarre names of some hostelries but the 'Slug and Lettuce' seems to have beaten them. There may be Lettuce in the salad in Albert Square but you would not wish to find it accompanied by a Slug. The 'Blue Parrot' suggests something exotic but probably not for eating. It is hard to imagine the connection between a Bat and a 'Thirsty Scholar'? Could it be that Bacardi is the source of the Bat genes implanted in students to enable them to walk about sending text messages without bumping into other people or street furniture? The Bat logo is part of a wall full of street art which creates an ambience popular with the customers but frowned upon by the authorities who want it removed from the Grade-II listed railway arch which is owned by Network Rail. Don't they understand that railway arches are not complete without graffiti?

Pub signs illustrate much of Britain's history, folklore and social customs. Many pay homage to Royalty, the Lord of the Manor, national and local heroes, sports or trades. Many of the images are derived from heraldic tradition, so animal images are common and there is a fine collection of signs with Horses, Lions, Eagles and other familiar beasts in a variety of colours from black to white with shades of grey, bay and exotic gold in between - but not silver? The 'Black Horse', the 'Black Lion' and the 'Eagle', all in Salford, incorporate their symbols, and even some of the equestrian trappings, within the structure of the buildings either on keystones over doors and windows or in terracotta panels. The 'White Horse' was the emblem of the King of Wessex. The 'White Lion' was incorporated in the badge of Edward IV, as the Earl of March, and is also the device of the Duke of Norfolk and others, so having your picture emblazoned on a pub sign is the equivalent of elevating an animal to the ranks of the aristocracy. This would not have impressed Karl Marx and Freidrich Engels who were reputed to have frequented the Hare and Hounds in Shudehill, but it has no sign to illustrate the pastimes of the aristocracy whether out of deference to them or in response to the ban on foxhunting?

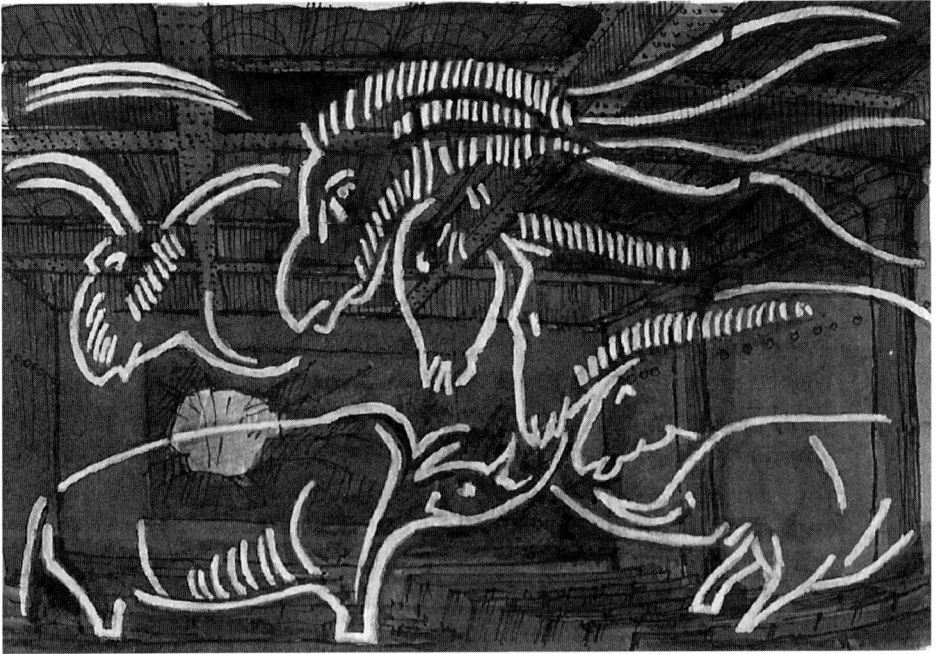

So how should we interpret the prehistoric cave paintings at Chauvet, shown in intimate detail in the 21st century film *'Cave of Forgotten Dreams'* in the cavernous space of the cinema at the Cornerhouse? The 32,000 year-old paintings show Lions, Rhinos, Hyenas, Horses, Mammoths and Cave Bears. According to Jean Clottes's definition in his book *'Cave Art'*, these drawings are not sophisticated representations made as 'the result of the projection of a strong mental image of the world in order to interpret and transform reality and recreate it in material form'. So, if not fine art, the drawings must at least be illustrations, but for what purpose? The draughtsmen were hunter-gatherers whose favourite food was Auroch, Deer, Horse and Bison but they had to compete with equally hungry Bears, Lions, Wolves and Rhinos for that food. In doing so they also had to avoid a host of predators who saw prehistoric Men as juicy delicacies in their part of the food chain. The cave could have been a temple controlled by a Shaman who called up the spirits to ensure a successful hunt by elimination of all this opposition? Or were these pictures on the walls for educational purposes, like the Second World War posters of silhouettes of friendly and enemy aircraft, so apprentice hunters attending this college would learn to recognise which animals could be caught for consumption and which must be avoided in case they had ideas of consuming unsuspecting hunters? Or could the pictures be no more than an elaborate menu in a very desirable restaurant at the height of fashion - and very much ahead of its time?

The Lord Mayor, at the opening ceremony in 1906, called the Victoria Baths 'Manchester's Water Palace'. A strict social division separated Males of different classes from Females who could mix freely. The baths closed in 1993 but are being restored to their former glory. The Second Class Males pool has been covered to create a venue for concerts, dancing, sports and other activities. Swimming has moved to the Aquatics Centre on Oxford Road.

EARTH
WATER
AIR
FIRE

The Fish Course

*A handsome punch bowl in earthenware, made around 1890
by William de Morgan and Halsey Ricardo, was decorated with
fish in painted copper lustre by Fred Passenger. They now
swim in their glazed cabinet in Manchester City Art Gallery
in the company of Pre-Raphaelite pictures and furniture.*

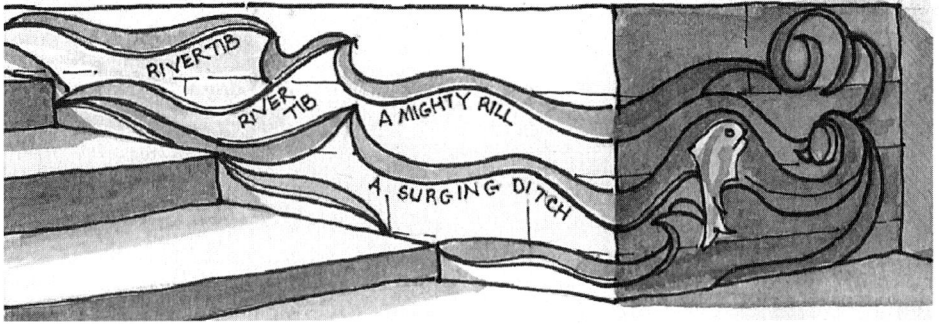

Rivers are natural waterways which need crossing points around which cities grow from humble beginnings. *'River Tib, River Tib, a mighty rill, a surging ditch'* runs the message etched into a concrete plinth in the Northern Quarter around an electricity substation, alluding to different currents, but nobody can remember that Tib Street marks the course of a river. When the Northern Quarter began its regeneration in the 1990s, they dreamed of creating an 'Urban Jungle' but they couldn't expose the river. So they gave it a monument instead. The sculpted waves, tumbling down the steps to break against the wall of the substation, evoke a romantic picture of the wilder aspects of the seaside rather than a gentle stroll along a river bank. Even in its heyday, it was rarely more than a dry bed into which effluent from fustian dyehouses was discharged along with general household waste. Downstream, in the 1700s, flagstones were placed to provide crossing points in Market Street for pedestrians who came from the 'cluster of pleasant homesteads along its banks', so the chances of seeing fish amongst this detritus would have been most unlikely. After it was culverted in 1783, in heavy rain it was said that you could hear it 'surging' below the cast iron access covers and it would frequently back up behind a dam of accumulated rubbish to cause flooding in New Cross, upstream of Great Ancoats Street. The stream still meanders in its conduit through the city, across Fountain Street, past the end of Tib Lane which had been a main thoroughfare to the banks of the river from which it took its name. It then crosses Princess Street to pass under the Town Hall, the Central Library and a corner of the Midland Hotel before crossing Lower Mosley Street and Great Bridgewater Street to join the Medlock near the former Gaythorn gasworks site where it had also been the natural boundary of the Roman settlement at Castlefield. The Bridgewater Canal gave birth to the Industrial Revolution which brought factories and mills to the city and added more pollution to the River Tib. Any hope of restoring it as a source of drinking water together with thoughts of a smiling fish leaping from the 'mighty rill' became, at best, a day dream.

The remains of the wholesale fish market became a garden centre in the Northern Quarter in the 1980s. Its later transformation into residential development retained the external walls with their sculpted panels over the former entrances, celebrating the activities of the fishermen whose catch came to the market with the occasional head of a fish visible, gasping its last breath in its struggle to escape. The retail market has become the Craft and Design Centre where artists and craftsmen have their studios. Kate Kelly's range of screen-printed fish, in various tableaux, celebrate the heritage of the building. The fishmongers have moved into the Arndale Market but their stalls are still reminiscent of a German tableau of 1890 in Mrs Greg's collection in the City Art Gallery. The amount of detail in its wax fish and game challenged the ingenuity of amateur model-makers who produced these items to teach young girls housekeeping skills. Thomas Horsfall opened the Ancoats Arts Museum in 1886 to educate the working classes to expect better living conditions and to encourage them to improve their grim surroundings in the houses clustered around the mills. His collection, also in the City Art Gallery, includes an Indian plate of 1884 with a bold drawing of a sailing boat and four Fish swimming beneath it. Similar designs are still being produced today.

The Ancient Worlds Gallery at the Manchester Museum demonstrates that dynamic forms of Fish have been used since the time of the ancient Egyptians in the design of cosmetic dishes and slate palettes for grinding make-up. It is unlikely that the model for a pressed glass posy trough in the City Art Gallery would have been a pike caught in the polluted waterways threading their way between the mills and factories in Ancoats where it was made by Molineaux, Webb & Company around 1885. To celebrate the 30th anniversary of the Craft and Design Centre, Lee Page Hanson created a ceramic vase with lustre decoration of Plaice, Cod, Haddock and Sea Bass inspired by the location of his studio opposite the stall of Ellen 'Nellie' Gibbons who was the only female trader working in the building when it was a fish and poultry market. The sign on her booth survives with the same tenacity as that of the Koi Carp which, legend has it, swam up the Yellow River waterfall and through the Dragon Gate to achieve success which it will pass on to the residents of the Tung Sing Housing Association in Princess Street where its image decorates metalwork grilles. A range of Lancastrian lustreware, decorated with silver and copper lustre Koi Carp in the style of the flowing brushwork of oriental calligraphy by Richard Joyce, was made by Pilkington's Tile and Pottery Company from 1908 to 1913. Ginger jars have lids adorned with small Carp, anticipating the growth of Chinatown adjacent to the City Art Gallery?

And the Lord said, I will destroy man whom I have created from the face of the earth; both man and beast, and the creeping thing, and the fowls of the air; for it repenteth me that I have made them'. This cry from the heart in the Book of Genesis, 6:7, led to the illogical decision to save some specimens from the Flood in the certain knowledge that by putting Man in charge of the operation, he would inevitably arrive back at the same corrupt point. We are now facing disasters caused by Man's poor management of the environment and there appears to be no more than a half-hearted recognition that it may be too late to attempt to correct the balance? However, it is not necessary to let modern politics get in the way of a good romantic folktale which has been used as a tool by the Shaman classes to support their religion and provide the inspiration for educational toys - to be played with only on Sundays, of course. The German Noah's Ark of painted softwood, in the City Art Gallery, was made around 1840. This ark has run aground in the Gallery of Craft and Design, allowing its animal passengers to stray into the garden of the Dolls' House next door. Both toys are part of Mrs Greg's bygones which she collected with a view to passing these on to museums to create children's corners. A love of models to a scale significantly less than life-size, acquired through the childhood pleasures of playing with these toys, stays for a lifetime and influences art and design according to the fashions of the day.

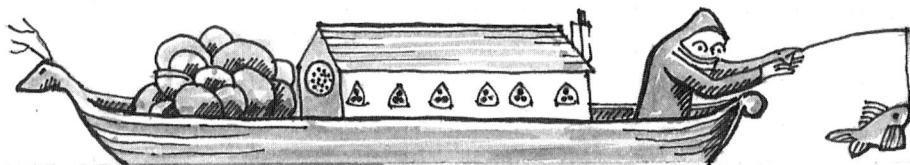

Fish are still present in the Northern Quarter which continues to exploit any connection in the cause of art: on the wall in the middle of Stevenson Square, the ephemeral graffiti incorporated a long boat with the characteristics of an ark. From its stern, a grotesque figure spent his time fishing - with surprising success.

The floor mosaics in the Victoria Baths include energetic fish swimming in the corridors with a border of Dolphins playing in the waves to lead other swimmers to the pool areas. But to lead audiences to other cultural activities, the Manchester Institution for the Promotion of Science, Literature and the Arts, designed by Charles Barry in 1824-35, graced its spacious auditoria with motifs connecting the different aspects of the various disciplines. The building is now the City Art Gallery and the frieze around the first floor Pre-Raphaelites Gallery has golden Carp swimming in formation along geometrical waves, restored along with the colour schemes of 1882 with elaborate stencilling and gilding.

95

Red Herrings

The Penguin pops up in various guises as a mascot or logo
for musical ensembles and has assumed a comic role along
with Daffy Duck and Pingu. The Penguin Café Orchestra,
visiting the Bridgewater Hall, had a statuesque bust of a
Penguin emerging from the top of their loudspeakers with
the rest of its body locked inside, making sure that this
unfortunate aquatic bird would never get airborne.

Definitions can be limiting when attempting to pigeon-hole certain creatures into fixed categories. The famous 'Bombay Duck', from the ethnic stores of Rusholme and Longsight, is not even a bird although, being a fish, it does live in Water in its natural state. Some birds are only honorary inhabitants of the element of Air, being flightless, but one particular specimen is more at home in the element of Water in its liquid or solid state. The ability of Penguins to walk on slippery ice makes them very comforting for children venturing onto this unfamiliar surface and in need of something secure for support amongst the madly whirling Christmas skaters on the seasonal ice rink in Spinningfields. Beneath the ice, in its natural habitat, the agility of the Penguin gives it the potential of a killer submarine, but it is still difficult to take these comical creatures seriously, even in an artistic context. At the Blank Space Gallery, a resin model of a Penguin by 'Wild at Art' has been decorated by European masters of the art of tattooing with patterns including Eagle wings so the bird could dream, at least, of taking flight. Another was painted by Krek of Manchester in the style of a flag so it might believe it could fly if only someone would tether it to the top of a flagpole?

Inhabitants from the warmer waters of the Nile have found comfortable surroundings in the Manchester Museum. Egyptian Crocodiles have been worshiped since the Pharaohs were in power, being the only animal without a tongue, because it has no need of speech, and having a thin transparent membrane over its eyes, so it can see under water. The Crocodile may well have become a symbol of deity amongst the ancient Egyptians who developed the accolade out of a strong sense of self-preservation? Even without a tongue, the Crocodile can 'moan' like a person in distress to entice unsuspecting victims to shed tears of pity, whereas the Crocodile sheds his own tears from a gland in the top of its mouth activated when he devours his prey. In the '*Unearthed*' exhibition at the Manchester Museum is a mummified baby Crocodile, but x-ray examination has revealed that it contains four skulls rather than a complete animal. Pedlars of souvenirs apparently have always been opportunists? However, the wrapping of decorative palm leaves makes patterns which reflect the Crocodile's natural textures. A more aggressive 'Crocidile' has been left by graffiti artists in Chinatown, but why he should be so angry is not clear. Perhaps the message has lost something in translation, although it reinforces Tom Lehrer's warning not to write on walls if you can't spell? The ultimate in aggression, however, is the Crocodile made from machine gun cartridge belts, trigger housings and pistol grips from Kalashnikov rifles, designed by artist Humberto Delgado as part of the Christian Council of Mozambique '*Transforming Arms into Ploughshares*' project in 2002, following the civil war 1976-92. It is on display in the Imperial War Museum North.

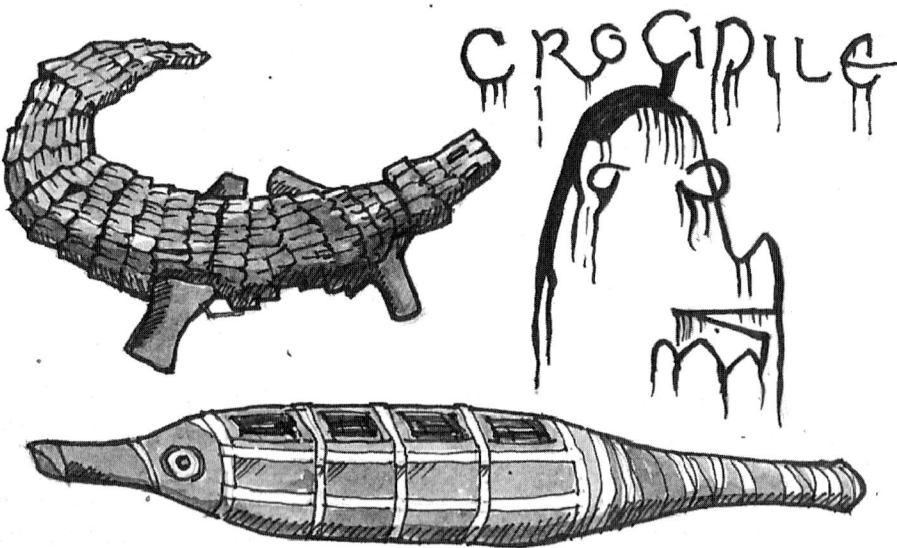

Manchester was not on the itinerary of the Beatles' Magical Mystery Tour, but a portrait of a handsome Walrus used to hang outside a bar in High Street. When it divided into two bars, one half lived on as 'Tusk' and the Walrus was left without his portrait. But some real Red Herrings live amongst the colourful restaurants along the Portland Street edge of Chinatown. Their glazed display cases, carefully placed at eye level, caused passers-by to look again to check that the lotus blossoms really did have eyes? They were not exotic blooms but large ceramic Koi Carp, complete with eyes, fins and tails curled around into a shape not unlike flowers, and the reflections of headlights of passing traffic danced like bubbles within their 'aquarium'. They have changed colour and migrated to a new home in Princess Street but seem to have lost their magic.

A weary young man carrying a sign gave people food for thought: 'Fish Pedicure' couldn't be a restaurant? Do marathon-running fish need a veterinary service? His message aimed to entice prospective customers to experience Turkish Garra fish nibbling away dead skin, aches and pains from tired feet. If these fish are related to Piranhas, the thought might deter the faint-hearted? In Manchester, you will always find something to challenge your perceptions of the world about you!

Whale Song

A Northern Quarter graffiti Whale hid discretely in an alcove on Kelvin Street, looking relieved to have escaped the attentions of the chef at the Sole restaurant at the other end of the road. The Whale disappeared but resurfaced briefly, run aground on the shutter of a shop in Tib Street. The restaurant sank without trace.

The skeleton of Manchester Museum's specimen of the Sperm Whale, *Physeter macrocephalus,* was acquired in 1898 and assembled by Harry Brazenor as one of their early acquisitions. The animal had been stranded in 1896 on the coast of Massachusetts where fishermen found it dying after it had come ashore on the ice, a tragic end for a creature which can dive to nearly 300 fathoms below the surface and swim at a stately four knots. Full-grown, it would be up to 60 feet long and weigh 44 tons. Its most famous relative was Moby Dick, the hero of Herman Melville's novel of 1851, based on records of real Whales which had caused death and destruction to whalers and their ships in the 1830s and 1840s. Captain Ahab's pursuit of the Whale in a war of attrition was told in a spellbinding adaptation for the stage of the Library Theatre where the intimacy of the space recreated the claustrophobic existence of the seafarers on a small whaling ship constantly in conflict with relentless seas. The strength and cunning of the Whale matched the obsessive zeal of the Captain as they battled with each other against the power of the sea and the wind, representing the dark perversity of life which inevitably ends in death. The relationship between Man, Whale and the Elements has now been reduced to Whale-watching as a staple product of ecotourism. People travel all over the Seven Seas to catch sight of a magnificent creature as it dives, raising its tail flukes like a piece of kinetic sculpture for a precious moment before it disappears beneath the calm surface in brilliant sunshine. The natural power of such an encounter could never compete with the total engagement of a memorable theatrical experience nearer home?

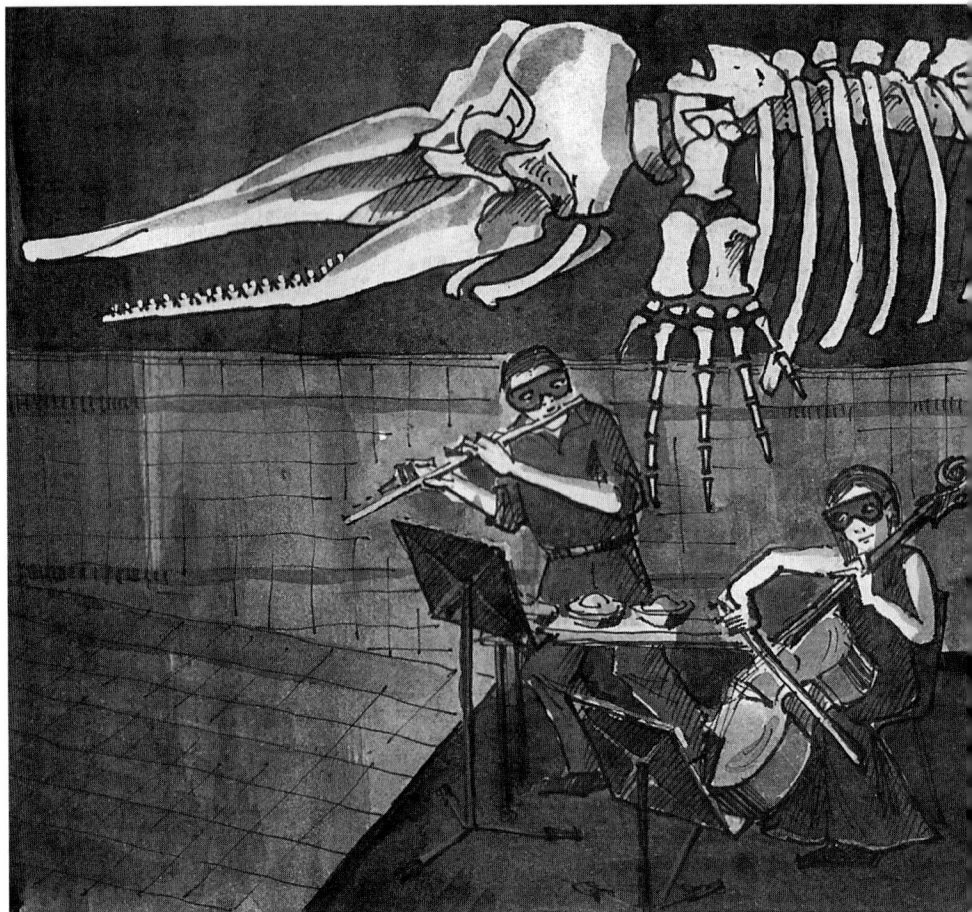

A dynamic expression of the Whale was presented by RNCM musicians as the final item of their inspired installation of *'Noise of Many Waters'* in the Victoria Baths. George Crumb's piece, *'Vox Balaenae'*, demonstrated all the nuances of the voice of the Whale which he had heard as a tape-recording of natural whalesong. With only a flute, cello, piano and minimal pieces of percussion, he devised subtle techniques of electronic manipulation of the sounds to develop incredible and beautiful effects which go beyond that natural voice and so become more like the Whale than the Whale itself. The visual delight of the performance took full advantage of its location in the First Class Men's pool, the largest space in this complex building, to pay appropriate homage to the majesty of the Whale as the light began to fade. As it progressed, the audience was drawn deeper and deeper into the world of the Whale by the dramatic lighting demanded by the composer, leaving the musicians stranded on a black island floating above the deep blue light

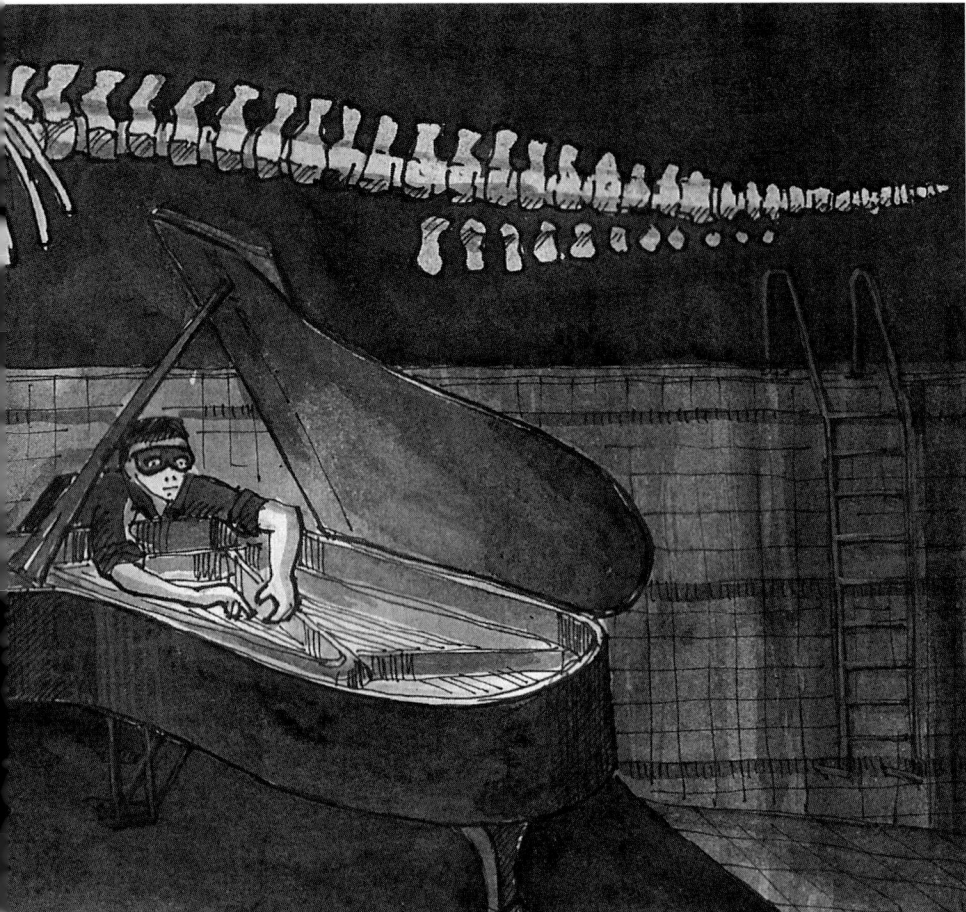

shimmering on the pool tiles beneath. Out of the darkness came the glow of illuminated music stands and the interior of the grand piano, lit so that the pianist, reaching into the depths of his instrument, could create a range of oriental notes by scraping, strumming and plucking its individual vocal cords with a variety of strange objects. The performers were all required to wear masks to symbolise the powerful, impersonal forces of the elements whilst the music built up to represent 'the larger rhythm of nature and a suspension of time', much as Captain Ahab and Moby Dick suspended reality in their desperately personal confrontation. As the final notes of the performance faded to absolute silence, the audience was spellbound and reluctant to disturb the tranquility with applause but, when it eventually started, it became as timeless as the music. This spiritually uplifting experience, which gave the Whale due deference as a truly magnificent creature, exceeded even the Whale-watching spectacle on the high seas.

Sea Creatures

The Great Hall of the Royal Exchange is a multi-purpose space which accommodates not only the auditorium of the main theatre but also space for musical events, exhibitions, café and bars, with display cabinets for the Craft and Design Shop whilst retaining features to celebrate its former life as a trading floor for cotton from all over the world.

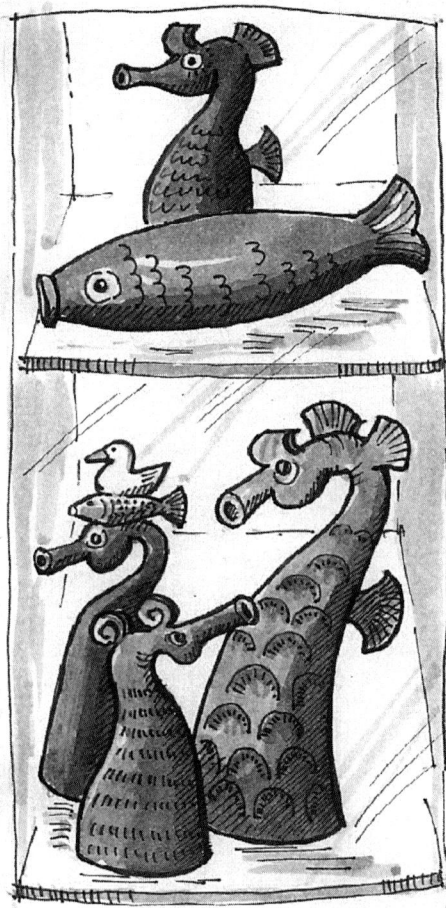

Abbey House on Mosley Street accommodates insurance companies and legal recruitment offices whose reception area is home to a magnificent collection of tropical fish. Their aquarium is a major engineering installation providing a spectacular attraction for visitors to the building and bait to catch the attention of passing children. The varieties of shape, size and colours of the fish create a kaleidoscopic underwater ballet of constant movement which is in sharp contrast to the static shoals of ceramic figures in the Great Hall of the Royal Exchange. Sue Crossfield's colourful marine creatures conjure up memories of her own childhood experiences of dipping into rock pools which she has translated into pieces with 'attitude', influenced by Modigliani, Picasso and Klimt. In this environment, it is the visitors who perform the ballet on their way into the theatre, exposed to the curiosity of myriad creatures watching every move from the waterless aquaria of the display cabinets around the concourse, hoping that they might get caught.

Archetypal flying animals land around the city every year to grace the Christmas Markets for those who are prepared to suspend their disbelief and accept that the Reindeers will take off at any moment? Lottie Smith's installation in the shop window of Fred Aldous in Stevenson Square was a triumph of artistic imagination and paper engineering.

EARTH
WATER
AIR
FIRE

Birds and Bees

The Beetham Tower, apart from being one of the tallest buildings in England, has a unique quality of humming in high winds from a particular direction, a sound which can be heard all over the city as a living symbol of the energy of a Beehive. It has become the pivot around which Manchester revolves, fixing the City to the Earth like a pin through an exotic Butterfly in a cosmopolitan collection of culture.

Bees which feature in mosaic floors of Waterhouse's Town Hall have been adopted as a symbol of the industry which created the prosperity of the city. In Manchester Day Parades, Bees enjoy the company of giant Dragonflies and Birds of Prey animated by expert puppeteers. 2012's theme of 'The Sky's the Limit' challenged designers to include anything which could fly, from Blackbirds to Balloons, Kestrels to Kites, Sparrows to Spaceships. The Indian community's handsome Peacock with its tailfeather display, marched with silver robotic birds and a flock of four-and-twenty Blackbirds hoping to avoid the attention of any piemakers. The Christie Hospital logo transformed windsock kites into Flying Fish. Two street-sweepers, disguised as enormous Bees, brought the proceedings to a memorable conclusion.

The Manchester Jazz Festival in Albert Square provided an opportunity to reunite some of the ephemeral participants of the Manchester Day Parade in a 'Junk Jam Session'. The Global Grooves band with their throbbing percussion and sonorous wind instruments, all fabricated from recycled materials and played by an army of grotesque animals, accompanied a pair of exotic winged creatures executing spectacular dance movements. A gilded Butterfly was seduced by the dark and mysterious colours of a huge Bat, their wings sweeping in time to the music. The carnival atmosphere was electric and a fitting reprise for the generous creative energy which went into the production.

Pre-Raphaelite artists favoured bright medieval colours, truth to nature, good materials and workmanship applied to pre-industrial values and took subjects from contemporary life, Biblical and literary sources rather than classical mythology. William Burges's furniture in the City Art Gallery combines these concepts in his writing desk, which was made by Gualbert Saunders in 1867. It is decorated with medieval scrolls inhabited by birds, lizards, butterflies, caterpillars and snails. Is this where Harvey Nichols found the inspiration for another 'different' display with moths, cockroaches and other bugs flying around giant light bulbs or lurking amongst fashionable ladies' shoes?

Messengers

Piccadilly Gardens has a resident population of Pigeons who wait patiently for tired shoppers, workers or visitors to share their snacks with them. They sit patiently like lost souls and occasionally take to the air when pursued by small children who enjoy the excitement of getting up close and personal with real birds and cannot resist the opportunity to generate a dynamic fly-past.

Many people believe that Pigeons are feral creatures who inhabit public spaces like undesirable vagrants because they don't realise that our breed has a long history of domestication and our presence used to be a measure of civilisation. The way people treat minorities today, whether that be Pigeons or vagrants, indicates that civilisation has slipped a bit. Hundreds of years ago our tender courtship rituals, cooing as we rub our necks together, made us symbols of love and fidelity, so having us around made people feel romantic and good about themselves - and civilised. You have to wonder, then, why they built us elaborate dovecotes like multi-storey hotels? If you checked in there you would be well looked after - until you finished up as somebody's dinner. I don't think that is the intention of the ornamental features around Islington Wharf and the Millennium Village? Those same people would take the credit for the idea of training us to use our natural skills in carrying messages, forgetting that it occurred to the Sultan of Baghdad centuries earlier. He thought he was so clever, but I don't suppose he was aware that we trained our first humans thousands of years before that. In fact, we Pigeons are capable of great feats of endurance. We enjoy racing to keep fit and to make sure our homing instincts are in proper working order, not like Man's fancy technology that sends people to the wrong place so they're late for appointments. You might not think that the rough Pigeon lofts on railway embankments or in back gardens could be thought of as 'home', but there's no place like it to athletes like us.

We've done our bit for Queen and Country whenever the military have needed our homing instincts in war zones. When a Pigeon is moved, after about six weeks it recognises its new location as home and will naturally return there. Pigeons became like pets to the poor infantrymen bogged down in the trenches during the Great War. There were 370 Pigeon-keepers in the field of battle in charge of a regiment of 20,000 Pigeons who showed extreme courage under fire. People call Pigeons 'Flying Rats', but they were proud to call Second World War soldiers 'Desert Rats', and those Rats were fighting in Egypt where the Delta Pigeon is known as a Bird of Paradise because the Nile Delta is Egypt's idea of Heaven on Earth as a respite from the hot desert sands. Fathi Hassan's drawings were part of the 'Faces and Voices' exhibition at the Rylands Library and he was told a story by his grandmother that a man went to Paradise where Birds kept him company. Pigeons and war heroes are treated like vermin as they potter about Piccadilly Station, and if it wasn't for lonely old people who live where they're denied the company of pets, we would never make contact with another species over a bag of dried crusts. The 'Authorities' are obsessed with droppings and tell everybody that we're insanitary and spread diseases. That's where the Rat connection comes from. I don't see old people seeking out Rats to feed with their breadcrumbs, but there was a plague of Rats in the Manchester Day Parade drawing attention to the need for people to stop spreading litter and do recycling instead. If they don't listen to Pigeons, perhaps the Rats can do better? I'll not hold my breath.

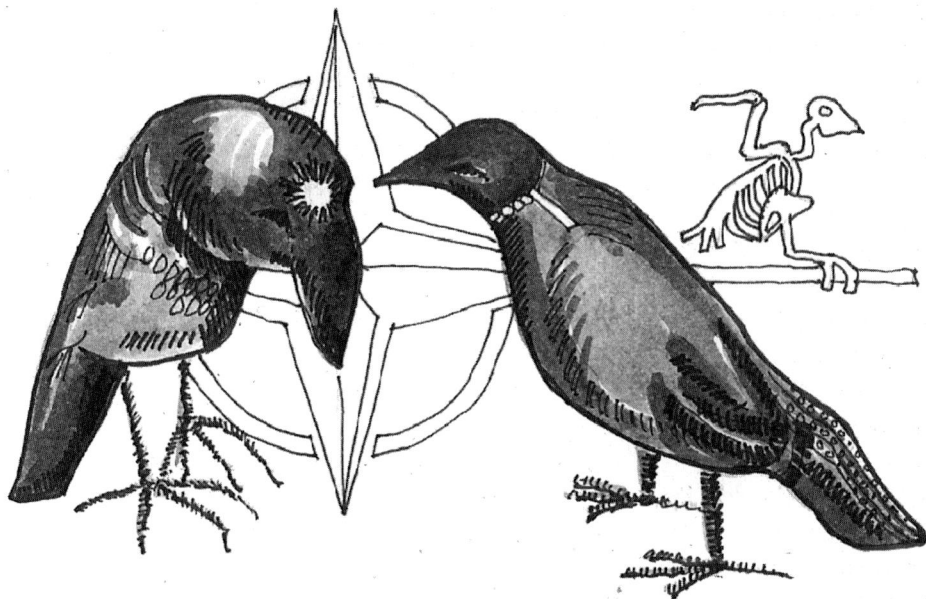

People complain if the streets are littered with rubbish but they forget who made the mess in the first place. They expect somebody to pick up whatever they drop as if their mothers are following right behind them. They don't seem to appreciate that Crows are experts in cleaning up carrion that nature generates as forlorn corpses run out of life. On the other hand, it's hard to take humans seriously when they believe the myth that Crows herald the arrival of guests, then at the same time fret about their blackness because they believe that Crows have a darker side to their character which brings some ill omen or even death? Not the most welcome of guests. The effigies in the Whitworth Art Gallery, made by Ruby Chisti in 2000 in the traditions of the Indian sub-continent using recycled materials, are a very appropriate reflection on the nature of Crows. Waste not, want not, that's what I say. But when it comes to dealing with the dead and the dying, you can't beat the Vultures. They circle around in the sky the minute they find some poor creature about to expire. I suppose you could compare their behaviour to that of the banks who, strangely enough, use Birds of Prey as their logo. Now, I wonder why they chose them? With a little imagination their Eagle emblems could easily become Vultures? The point was made by Mexican artist Minerva Cuevas in the 'Landings' exhibition at the Cornerhouse in a piece with the skeletal form of a Vulture perched on the logo of NATO whose 'official military doctrine reserves for itself the rights to use nuclear weapons, posing the risk of a Nuclear Winter, a global environmental holocaust'. Who do they expect will clear up that mess?

It's funny how people depend on Pigeons to deliver messages at all sorts of levels, but they don't seem to have the sense to work things out for themselves. Take the plastic Pigeon that took pride of place in the 'Everything Must Go' presentation at the Chinese Arts Centre in 2011. The exhibition and workshop drew attention to the wasteful accumulation of unwanted articles in a throwaway society, along with the low wages earned by exploited workers and the rapidly rising price of gold in an economic crisis. There were enough dots there for people to join up but how many of them are capable of making the right connections - and then try to do something about it? The plastic Pigeon was only the messenger but the artist Han Feng sent his own message in another exhibition. He made a leather flying jacket and shoes for birds as a metaphor to reflect the human world. However the birds resisted his temptation to opt for glamorous outfits and were not prepared to sacrifice their natural ability to fly just for the sake of appearance. Birds have more sense than humans and visitors to the Contact Theatre could trust the small ceramic Pigeons resting on the steel beams above the foyer. They knew they could sit below them without fear of being bombarded by droppings as these birds had been part of an art installation. A few have flown away but the rest remain with bits of other exhibitions to haunt the space with memories of previous lives.

Pigeons are always ready to help scientists who strap equipment to our backs to collect samples of air pollution while they track us with a GPS system. But we're dull and grey, so our contribution to the development of science, politics and engineering goes unnoticed. If we were colourful and liked to show off, we might have found a place in Kate Plumtree's exhibition 'Worn to be Wild' at Ordsall Hall. She expressed the character of British birds - and a few mammals - exploiting the colours and textures of various materials, finished with dyes, paints, prints, embroidery and quilting to evoke the form of the creatures in a range of costumes from different periods. The Great Crested Grebe and the Pheasant represented the 1600s, the Kingfisher and the Swan the 1700s, the Heron and the Pipistrelle Bat the 1800s and a Golden Eagle evokes the 1930s.

Dawn Chorus

A sentinel Pigeon sitting high on a roof gable in Catlow Lane must surely be a refugee from a cartoon film, disguised as a cementitious 'bobble hat' draped over the ridge finial? And in strong winds his head moves from side to side like a weather vane as he scans his horizon. In the Northern Quarter, you can never be quite sure of the origin of apparently innocent creatures who might just be art installations.

The high-definition, vibrant notes of a lone Blackbird rang out over Tib Street. Other members of the dawn chorus had decided that the summer solstice could manage well enough without their contribution at such an ungodly hour. As his ambitious song was augmented by the descant drone of the mechanical street-sweeper and the intermittent chant of a distant car-alarm, they had wisely calculated that their best efforts would never be heard anyway. The Blackbird made a tactical withdrawal as a hostile cascade of breaking glass crashed into the hollow depths of the recycling truck. There is always a point when you know you can't win, but the flock of blue Delft ceramic Pigeons, clinging in formation to the staircase tower of the car park, remained poised to take off at a moment's notice, ready to claim their share of any excitement, to make a pre-emptive strike against raucous urban Starlings or to challenge the rasping police helicopter on its early morning manoeuvres. The trouble with dawn in midsummer was that nobody seemed to realise what time it was? As the sun climbed above the castellated horizon of office blocks and chimney pots, it would not be long before the whole Northern Quarter would be wide awake and any semblance of 'peace' would be lost. A sergeant Pigeon, with striped bars on his wings, was already trying to marshal his troops on the parapet above Matt and Phred's jazz club but they were only interested in making a different sort of music with their sweethearts.

A pair of Magpies, scratched their way over the roof slates, bickering, chattering, clattering, supposedly foretelling disagreement between man and wife. Is that what they were doing, perched on the huge red letters on the Thomas Street windows of Oipoloi with two more of their kind? One for sorrow, two for joy, was good to start the day but now we had three for a girl and four for a boy. Well, the men's outfitters selected Magpies as their emblem because of their attraction to shiny things - so the wicked birds stole the 'H' of the shop's name! It still has its identity with the Greek concept of 'many', although if John Dryden is to be believed, 'the masses are sometimes in the right, sometimes in the wrong; their judgement is a mere lottery'. Let's hope that Oipoloi's democratic customers are discerning. But round the corner in Oak Street there are four more Magpies on the other window: five for silver, six for gold, seven for a secret never to be told, eight for a wish. Be careful what you wish for, especially if it involves a bird with a dubious character, mischievous, thieving, likely to be associated with witchcraft. Listen carefully. If these Magpies were chattering with a Chinese accent, they could have been heralding the arrival of guests, just like the Crows who belong to the same family. They could even be the guests themselves and have come to visit the Parrots in Tib Street? Red terracotta avian figures perched on the window cills, stare disconcertingly into the room beyond. They have no accent. They do not speak in any language. They neglected to learn that which would have come so easily when they were chicks, like human chicks who discover too late that learning is for the young and becomes much more difficult when they get older. The Parrots ignore the world in the street below, not for them the mystical science of tweets and texts. Since the Canaries flew away from the building opposite, the Parrots are now the only reminder of the myriad pet shops which, half a century ago, clustered together in Tib Street like an oriental bazaar.

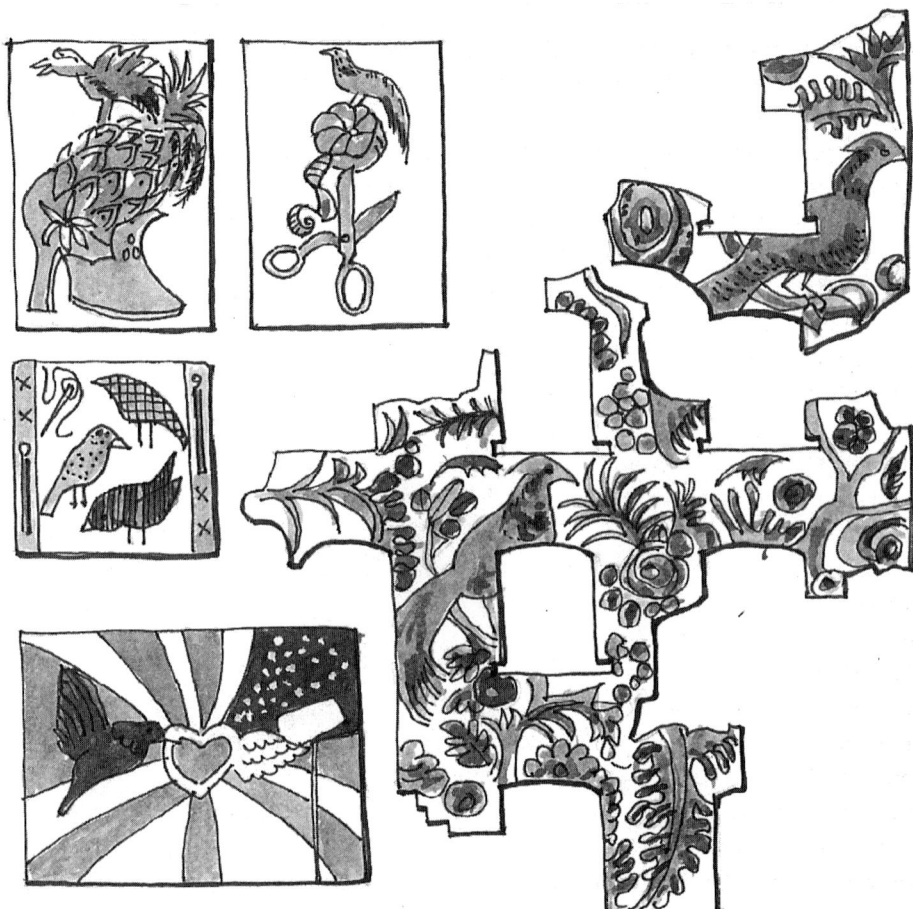

The Parrots are not the only exotics in the Northern Quarter. Others remain from the major installation of artwork throughout the area in the mid 1990s. Humming Birds try to persuade us to feel just a bit tropical. The tiles embedded in the walls of the houses along Martlesham Walk adjacent to the Craft and Design Centre were part of that project and reflect the fashions being created in the studios. A Humming Bird perches on a pineapple in a shoe, an exotic Pheasant sits on an orange balanced on a pair of scissors, and humble local species are relegated with needle and thread to the workshop wing of the dress department. More Pheasants live in a ceramic mural in Jubilee Walk, evoking patterns which might have been produced by calico printers who occupied this site, inspired by exotic creatures from the pet shops which existed in Tib Street. There are also suggestions of oak trees which would have lined the banks of the River Tib before the town spread outwards. An ephemeral Humming Bird landed on the shutter of American Graffiti on Hilton Street but has gone to search elsewhere for his friends.

The village elders perch quietly in John Street on redundant cast iron brackets, retired from their work supporting a fire escape staircase. The ceramic birds, with their metallic tail feathers blowing in the wind, sit in the same place every day, like the inmates in a retirement home. Their habitual daily routine is absolutely inviolable in this cloistered and cliquish society: four Toucans monopolise one bracket whilst two more of their kind consort with a pair of exotic Pheasants, and yet another is obliged to keep company with two Crested Cranes. Two Owls listen patiently to the complaints of a lone Pheasant who has fallen out of the love triangle on the neighbouring bracket. These are not Mancunian birds. They could be illegal immigrants, asylum-seekers, the under-cover remnants of an advance guard sent to create a bridgehead for the occupation of the city on Christmas Day when it's completely deserted? It's rumoured that, some years ago, there used to be many more in their party but they have disappeared, one by one, lost through neglect, decay or, perhaps, kidnapping? These survivors must rely on the human residents' habit never to raise their eyes above shop windows, so no-one sees them, even in broad daylight. They show no sign of hostility, no Hitchcockian tendencies to swoop down to peck out the eyes of those who see nothing anyway. Do these geriatric creatures have a sinister purpose or are they merely hoping to lull us into a sense of security which only they can disturb at any time?

The disturbing image of the Strawman in Edge Street has been obliged to seek alternative employment in pastures new. Although frighteningly similar to a Crucifix, it was no deterrent to the Pigeons which sat on his pinioned arms whilst keeping well clear of the thorns wound about his hat. They took no part in the dawn chorus, any more than the Pigeon posted on his gable vantage point high above Catlow Lane, determined to detect any intruders passing below. Has he noticed that some of the older members of the community have made their last contribution to the dawn chorus and have passed into another world? An installation in the staircase of the Craft and Design Centre gathers their pathetic ceramic corpses on a ledge where, having come to the end of their useful lives, they appear frozen in time, their terminal decay arrested. The Crows can't help them any more. Will the people passing on their way to and from the upper studios contemplate the fragility of their own lives? The specimen of a Passenger Pigeon in the new 'Nature's Library' Gallery in the Manchester Museum is displayed in a similar pose to draw attention to scientific studies endeavouring to understand the dynamics of the process of extinction. The Northern Quarter has its own dynamic and the Birds are an essential component of that - but without thoughts of extinction.

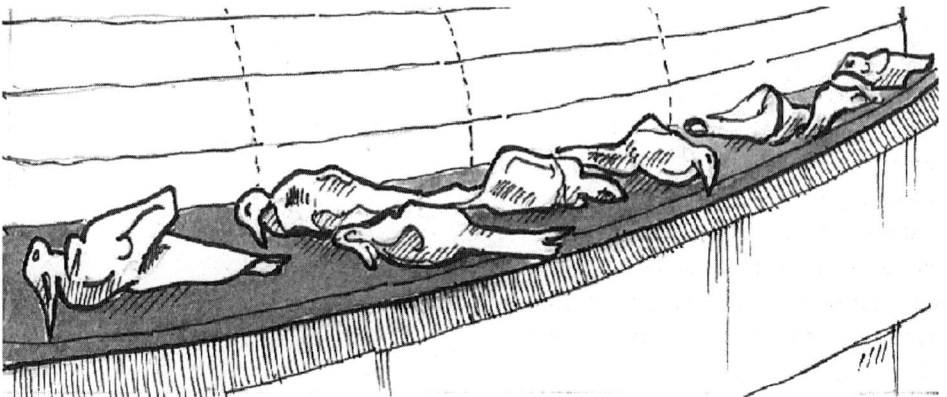

Seasonal Visitors

Throughout the year, Manchester attracts visitors to celebrate the different seasons with markets of food, crafts and fashions which weave their way from one open space to another. Piccadilly Gardens in 2011 was graced with a pair of giant Reindeer woven from threads of tiny lights to herald the Christmas Fair.

In a welcome display of summer sunshine, St Ann's Square became a Moroccan bazaar with traders, dressed in traditional robes, offering glass lanterns and lamps, ceramic incense-burners, tile mosaic inlaid in table tops, carved wooden gifts, hand-woven rugs and carpets, soft camel leather ottoman hassocks and slippers with turned up toes, full of eastern promise, food and hospitality. Amongst all this activity were white-painted metal Storks with arched necks bent low, listening to the pulsating drums. As the sun went down, the copper Rooster would migrate south to herald the dawn in a warmer place. It was Albert Square's turn to become a magical place for the Autumn Mela to celebrate the Diwali 'Festival of Lights' with its procession of lanterns to remember Prince Rama's return to Ayodhya with his wife Sita. Lord Krishna and his atavars in the shape of Eagles and Cranes triumphed over the demon Ravan in an event which combined religious purpose and sheer festive enjoyment, shared by various faiths with their own interpretations.

Whilst people sought thrills on the Wheel of Manchester, trying to imagine what it would be like to fly, Peregrine Falcons returned to the city to build their nest on a ledge on the cliff face of a tower block. The only difference between this and their natural habitat was the voyeuristic presence of telescopes in Exchange Square trained on these magnificent birds wheeling above the Arndale Centre. From the first sighting of the parent birds to the departure of a new family, web-cam surveillance enabled conservationists to give regular updates on the progress of the chicks, reported through various media. Excitement built as four fledgling Falcons prepared to make their first flight in their training to transform them into predators capable of achieving speeds of 200 miles per hour. This fascination with Birds of Prey goes back to the ancient Egyptians who put god-like models of Hawks in their tombs. A display in Ordsall Hall showed that, in medieval England, the Law of Ownership determined that only the King could hunt with a Gyrfalcon, a Priest with a female Sparrowhawk and a Servant with a Kestrel. Anyone hunting with a bird above their station would be punished by cutting off the offender's hand.

During the 2011 Chorlton Arts Festival, a flock of life-size 'Culture Vultures' crash-landed menacingly amongst the trees of the Ivy Green Nature Reserve. Children from Brookburn Primary School, with artist Jude Macpherson, made the birds to demonstrate society's attitude to 'transient cultural artefacts in a digital society'. The installation gave them the intimate tactile experience of making sculptural forms from recycled materials to explore texture, colour and, most of all, character. The multi-ethnic environment of Chorlton has no Towers of Silence where deceased Parsees can be left for the birds to perform their essential last rites to welcome the deceased into the afterlife. A warmer form of welcome was devised for their exhibition at the City Art Gallery by the Cumbrian Multicultural Women's Network. The Ultimate Holding Company made a video installation in which the ladies held up prints of bird drawings by John Powell Jones in the Airport Arrivals Hall to receive visitors from abroad. However, they had no response, suggesting that the birds might have been diverted to another airport?

Waterfowl

The Canada Goose has taken up residence on the rivers and waterways of the canal network that thread their way through Manchester so they can take advantage of any cultural opportunities the city has to offer and have concentrated their numbers around the Portland Basin Museum.

Most birds inhabit the element of Air, with occasional contact with Earth, but some groups can live in other elements. Most notable are the Waterfowl, as much at home on Water as in the Air - or even on dry land. It's wonderful to have such a choice. Geese are a very distinguished kettle of feathers. They have a degree of elegance, vigilance and those of my acquaintance are always prepared to make a lot of noise on that account. The arrival of Canada Geese from the New World in the 17th century set them on a path to success in interbreeding with local species, but this is now frowned upon as being the cause of the decline of those species. Why the locals can't take a feather out of their book and learn how to survive is quite beyond me as, indeed, it appears to be beyond their detractors. Charles Darwin's observations led to theories that the fittest of any species will be best able to survive and Canada Geese seem to have proved his point very well. But to get fit it is necessary to take exercise which involves a little more than marching about with placards and banners. In the People's History Museum, the debate over Women's right to have a parliamentary vote is illustrated by a postcard, produced in 1913, with images of Geese. Why Geese? Well, it was circulated by Men, who were opposed to the Women's Suffrage Movement, to suggest that Women were only politically active if they were unable to find a suitable husband - or, as they saw it, a 'Propagander'. Hrmmph! Proper Geese don't need to be patronised just to make pompous human beings feel good about themselves by mixing clever metaphors and awful puns - especially at the expense of their female companions!

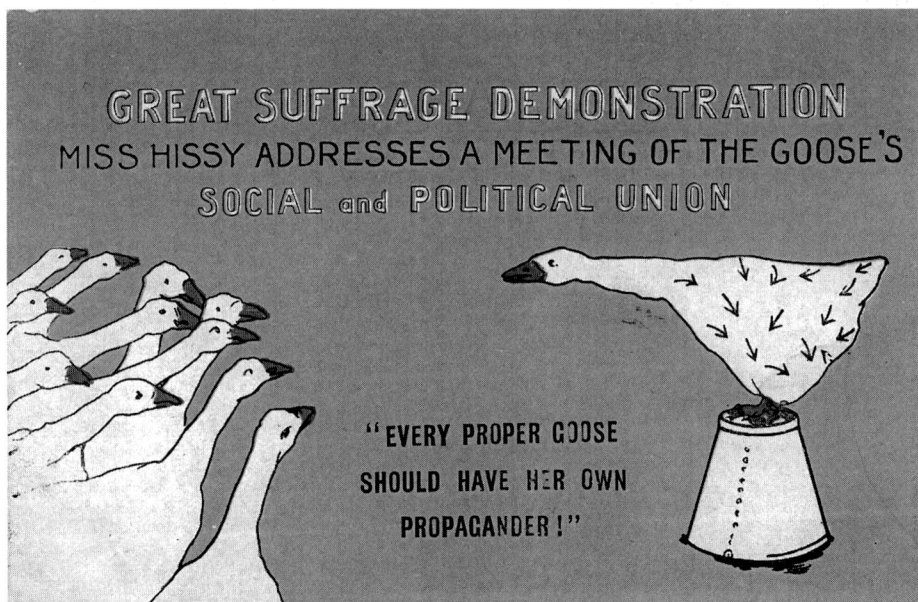

Reproduced by permission of People's History Museum

Portraits of Geese from the distant past still hang outside local hostelries, but their stories seem to be lost in the culverts of history. So if you're perched comfortably, I'll exercise a little licence to set one down as I wouldn't want it to be forgotten. Once upon a time, there was an Apothecary's shop on the corner of Phoenix Street in the town centre. One bitterly cold morning, the Apothecary opened his door and found a Goose sitting on the step. The nearby River Tib had frozen solid, in spite of the efforts of the waterfowl paddling around all night in the freezing water to keep a small patch open. The Goose was very tired and in need of shelter. Times were hard and the Apothecary's wife thought that this gift of fresh meat would ease their hardship. She began rattling pans in the kitchen and perusing her recipes. The Apothecary was not happy to commit the bird to the cooking pot and endured his wife's admonition and her abuse and her sarcasm for his weakness, as she put it. She told him that they could not afford to feed another mouth so, if he was not prepared to eat the Goose, he must share his own food with the bird. So the Apothecary shared his own meagre rations with the Goose which followed him everywhere because it knew that if the Apothecary's wife caught it alone, it would be in the pot in the twinkling of an eye, no matter what the Apothecary said.

When the ice melted, the Goose showed no inclination to return to its watery habitat. It had become firmly imprinted on the Apothecary and they became inseparable. The Goose slept in a box in the small yard behind the shop and every night the Apothecary would lock the back door and slip the key into the pocket of his nightshirt so that his wife would not be tempted to indulge in any late night culinary exercises which required a Goose. The Goose was extremely thankful for its master's thoughtfulness. Then, one dark night, the town was consumed by madness. People were rushing back and forth, shouting, smashing windows, stealing food, clothes, anything of value. The town watchmen set up a hue and cry and did their best to apprehend anyone burdened with loot. The Goose sat anxiously in its box looking at the orange glow in the sky which meant that something was on fire in Market Street. Suddenly, a bag flew through the air and crashed to earth next to its box as two hands and a dark hood appeared over the wall. The Goose could not let an intruder into the yard so it made a noise loud enough to wake the dead! As the Apothecary's bedroom window was flung open, the hood and the hands disappeared back out of sight. The Apothecary came downstairs to find the Goose guarding the bag. Inside was a hoard of gold and silver ornaments which the Apothecary recognised as belonging to a notable Alderman for whom he supplied restorative potions. In the morning he returned the treasures to their grateful owner who gave the Apothecary a handsome reward. The Apothecary's wife was very happy and promised that she would never again be tempted to cook the Apothecary's Goose.

PADDYS GOOSE

The Apothecary's name was Paddy and long afterwards, when the town grew bigger, all the old houses and shops were swept away to make way for a new town centre. The Apothecary built a new shop on another site in Bloom Street and this eventually became an inn which was known as the 'Famous Paddy's Goose'. But the innkeeper and his wife had no children and did not pass on the story, so very soon no-one remembered why the Goose was Famous - and Paddy was forgotten. The present innkeeper could only recall that during the Second World War the inn became a place where prostitutes took advantage of American Servicemen, so the title should have been changed to the 'Infamous Paddy's Goose'. But it was not the Goose that was infamous!

Another inn, the 'Shakespeare', was built on the corner of Phoenix Street in 1771 and decorated with coloured carvings taken from the 'Shambles' in Chester. These illustrate scenes of medieval life, pastimes and everyday activities and one of the characters is caught in the act of stealing a Goose. The punishment for such a crime is not shown, presumably to avoid deterring customers to the inn? Civilisation has moved on since then and the development of medical science has produced a bewildering collection of pills and tablets which have overtaken the craft of the Apothecary, sadly, not always to good effect. So there are no Apothecaries' shops left, although the inns all over the city dispense restorative potions which are still effective for some conditions.

Many years ago, a High Court Judge thought he would like to be reincarnated as a Duck because they have beautiful children. He should have taken a longer view as all children start out beautiful but even the fluffy bobbing offspring of Ducks grow up into audacious and raucous creatures in adolescence and even worse as they grow older. The Chinese took Ducks very seriously 1500 years ago and placed ceramic models in tombs in recognition of their fidelity so that the deceased would have good company in the afterlife and the well-fed figure in the City Art Gallery might also suggest that the Duck would become part of the food supply to sustain the departed in the manner to which they had become accustomed? The windows in the Chinatown cafés, with their racks of crispy Ducks, inspired artists Lisa Cheung and Jennifer Tarrant who made the '*Bliss 2004*' chandelier for the Chinese Arts Centre. A metal rail snaking across the ceiling of the shop was hung with hand-blown glass shapes of crispy Ducks and cooking utensils to reflect the vibrancy and rich atmosphere of Chinese markets and restaurants from around the world, bringing together exotic and everyday items. The Tudor kitchen in Ordsall Hall has similar racks of game birds awaiting their turn for the pot in a celebration of food as an art form in its own right - even as raw material.

Comical wood carvings from plant roots in the Piccadilly Gardens market, like movie cartoons, exploit the Duck's light-hearted air of happiness. However, the birds are clever enough to keep a clear route to open water so they can retreat safely from earth-bound predators. Notable exceptions have been known to lose their presence of mind, like the Duck quacking from the middle of the pond but getting so excited that it jumped out of the water into the jaws of the Wolf which was then captured by Peter in Prokofiev's musical fairy tale. There's always one! You wouldn't catch a Goose behaving in such a stupid manner. The parade of Ducks etched into the stone parapet of the Bridgewater Viaduct were on their way to the Good Friday Duck Race on the River Irwell in Spinningfields. Battling with the current against the wind, they were surely hoping that they might win a prize of a new residence painted in the primary colours of traditional waterways decoration? The Ducks should try to imagine that the canal is really a moat and the aristocracy might claim the cost of their maintenance on Parliamentary Expenses?

The general discontent with our own view of ourselves gives rise to aspirations that all our Geese will become Swans, especially children who are perceived by their parents to be paragons. But if those children turn out to be Geese after all, they quite clearly didn't live up to expectations. In a crisis of identity, a Swan survived by singing sweetly so that a more raucous Goose would finish up in the cooking pot in its place. The myth of its performing a 'Swansong' before it dies is hopelessly romantic. Like so many others, Aesop's Raven was overwhelmed by the beauty of the Swan. In fact, it was so awestruck that it spent all its time washing its feathers, hoping to turn their blackness into white. This obsession caused it to forget to take its food from the neighbourhood altars, so it died of starvation. The 21st century film of the 'Black Swan' explored the obsessive theme in the behaviour of a ballet dancer who was desperate to play the parts of both a White Swan and a Black Swan because she believed that she possessed the skill to interpret the individual characteristics of both birds. Her belief was so intense that the darker side of her own character took over and she grew feathers - ominous black feathers. The Raven might have understood this? As a Mancunian, I appreciate the celebration of the species found, naturally enough, in Swan Street. An elegant sculpture of a Swan graces the tympanum above the entrance to Swan Buildings and a modern stencilled pattern of stylised Swans lines the wall of the tunnel into the courtyard beyond. These parents must be proud that their clever offspring has opened the Cygnet sandwich bar next door.

Swans are certainly the most regal of the Waterfowl and must be relieved when their own 'ugly ducklings' blossom into elegant birds which are, paradoxically, symbolic of light as well as melancholy and death. These attributes have inspired poetry, literature, art and music throughout history and legends from ancient Greece have influenced the works of Spenser, Shakespeare, Coleridge and Tchaikovsky. They have also provided the motif for a family of these stately birds living in the refurbished landscape around Ordsall Hall. The building is an organic piece of English architecture with parts surviving from 1360, augmented by Tudor and Victorian extensions. The Hall is located on a bend in the River Irwell which, in the 1700s, had clear waters filled with jumping trout, grayling and salmon. For 500 years the building was surrounded by a moat which is now delineated by a vestigial dry depression in the lawns of the restored gardens and this is graced by a pair of large wooden Swans with a line of Cygnets extended behind them, adding a set of 21st century garden ornaments to the historic time line of the Hall. On a more intimate scale, the City Art Gallery has a pair of small boxes in Chinese jade from 1895 with elegant carved Swans, but no Cygnets.

Life and Death

The Demoiselle Crane, faithfully prepared by the taxidermists, occupies pride of place in a cabinet in the Living World Gallery of Manchester Museum. It symbolises the devastation caused by war with evermore powerful weapons to wreak havoc on people, all other living organisms and the planet itself.

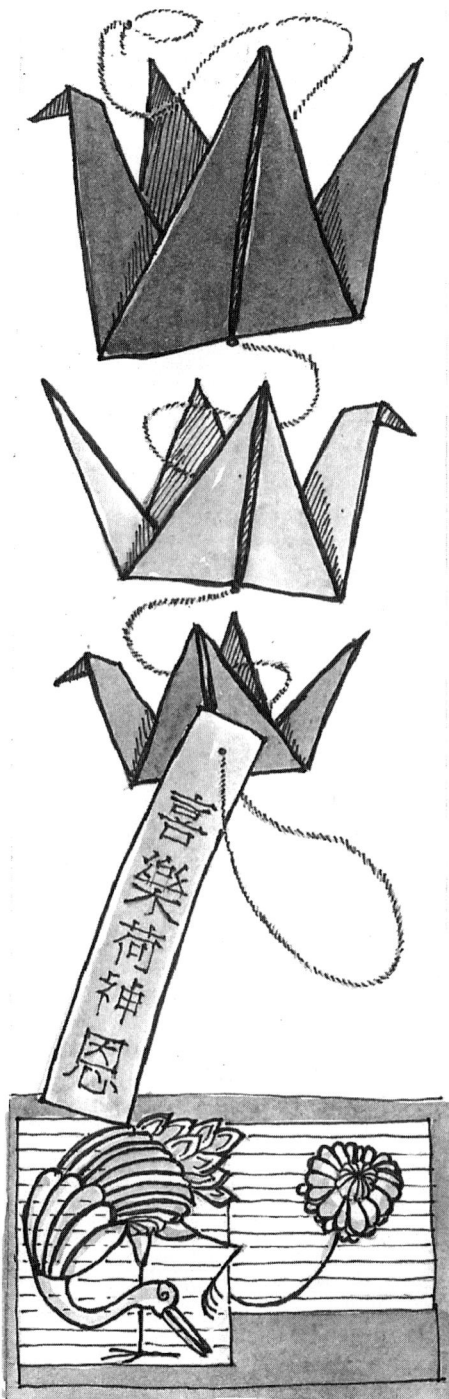

The devastation of war is represented in the Manchester Museum by a display of hundreds of small white origami Cranes which, in Japan, are a symbol of long life. These illustrate the story of Sadako Sasaki, a young girl who was exposed to the fallout from the atomic bomb dropped in 1945 on Hiroshima. So that she might recover from the resulting radiation sickness, she followed the stipulations of the legend to make her wish come true and folded 1000 paper Cranes. Helped by her school friends, she wrote 'Peace' on the wings of every bird so that they might fly all over the world to deliver her message that such an awful thing should never be allowed to happen again. Sadly, she died at the age of 12 after ten years of suffering but the Demoiselle Crane on which her birds were based has now become an international symbol of peace. The same models of paper cranes are used as icons to celebrate Chinese New Year, bringing salutations from the Gods with wishes of happiness and good luck as strings of birds in different colours and sizes, like a kite tail with a message inscribed on a final streamer, to harmonise the cultures of Buddhism and Christianity for a large cosmopolitan population as well as the tourists who make their own pilgrimage to enjoy the colourful festivities in Chinatown. The Tung Sing Housing Association have incorporated metalwork images of the same bird on their building in Princess Street to ensure that the residents will also enjoy the blessings it will bring throughout the year.

137

Life is too short and there is never a good time for it to end, whether it means the loss of a genius in his prime, a youth denied the opportunity to fulfil his potential, or a whole species on the verge of extinction. The memorial to Chopin, erected in Deansgate, commemorates the bicentenary of the composer's birth and refers to his Gala Concert in the Gentlemen's Concert Hall in Manchester in 1848. In spite of being extremely ill, Chopin endeared himself to his audience by performing, only a year before he died at the age of 39. Commissioned by the Chopin Memorial Monument Committee and the Polish Consulate, with Bruntwood as principal sponsor, the design by Polish sculptor Robert Sobocinski shows Chopin at his piano, gazing at his muse Baroness Aurore Lucile Dupon, against the backdrop of a battle scene representing the Polish fight for Freedom, all carried on the spreading wings of an Eagle in flight as a symbol of Poland. The romanticism of this sculpture contrasts with the commercialism of the Armani store logo on the other side of Deansgate. Its motif of a predatory Eagle, traced in fluorescent lighting tubes across its windows, is reflected in the windows of the buildings around the statue, epitomising the dead hand of capitalism?

'Rory's Bench' in the Fletcher Moss Botanic Garden in Didsbury is another memorial to a life ended too soon. Rory McGowan was a young schoolboy, tragically killed in a road accident in 2004. His classmates arranged a concert and a doughnut-eating competition to raise funds for artist Jason Thompson to create a seat decorated with Rory's favourite characters from books and television series which together form a menagerie of birds, animals, fish and spacemen, all carved into the wooden seat with cast metal supports in the form of a giant bat at one end and a grotesque cartoon figure at the other. To celebrate the bicentenary of Charles Darwin's birth in 2009, the 'Extinked' exhibition at the Manchester Museum identified one hundred threatened species, including birds, marine creatures, amphibians, reptiles, invertebrates, mammals, plants and fungi in an attempt to arrest the slide into oblivion of these species from the real world. Artist Jai Redman made ink drawings from taxidermists' specimens and herbarium sheets in the Museum's collections which included the Western Capercallie, *Tetrao urogallus*. Individual images were then tattooed onto a hundred volunteers by artists from Ink vs Steel to create ambassadors for conservation in a unique social experiment to draw attention to the perilous state of each endangered species.

The City Council's Peace Memorial Competition in 1986 was won by Barbara Pearson with her '*Messenger of Peace*' which became the centrepiece of the Peace Garden in St Peter's Square. It was removed to make way for the redevelopment of the Central Library and the Town Hall which includes proposals for the Metrolink Second City Crossing and relocation of the Cenotaph to be completed by 2016. The '*Messenger*' had her retinue of bronze Pigeons which she instructed to deliver her communications and it must be hoped that these homing Pigeons will return as part of the project? The runner-up was '*Doves of Peace*' by Michael Lyons with their swirling white wings rising up against the background of the rusting surface of the steel cladding of the extension to the People's History Museum. The Museum's exhibits tell the story of working people and their struggle for political representation but also deals with the politics of conflict in defence of those democratic rights. War and its consequent human losses are an indication of how badly their leaders, in pursuit of their own agendas, have failed the population who have paid a very high price for the freedom of their fellow men. This becomes increasingly significant in the face of disproportionate power which now rests in the hands of leaders, elected and unelected, who must surely be due for a reminder from the people that democracy itself is now under pressure?

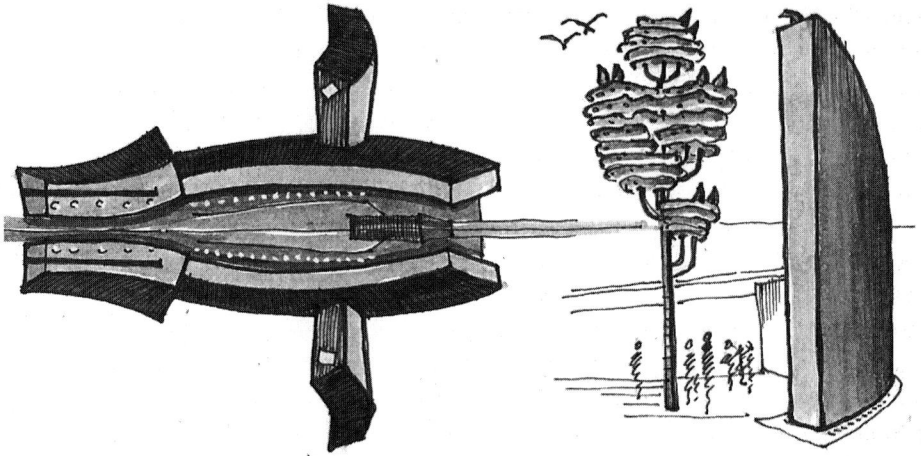

The Imperial War Museum North is itself a monument to the futility of war. The organisation was established to honour those who lost their lives in the Great War and records conflicts from around the world since then. Architect Daniel Libeskind's design assembles the shards of a broken sphere to represent a world shattered by confrontations on Land, on Water and in the Air. The concept of War itself adds Fire with a red light high in the Air Shard reflected in the Manchester Ship Canal to link this with the medieval understanding of the Elements. Ironically, the advanced technology of modern warfare finds that it is no match for the medieval techniques still practised by Third World guerilla forces which can only be defeated by disproportionately excessive force causing high levels of collateral damage. The 'Tree of Remembrance' by Wolfgang and Heron, erected in 2005 in Piccadilly Gardens, deals with that issue and honours the memory of the Civilians who lost their lives in Manchester during bombardment in the Second World War. Their sacrifice in keeping services going or manufacturing supplies for the armed forces, while their loved ones went off to confront the enemy, was far more devastating to those soldiers returning home after surviving the mayhem of the front lines to be confronted by the loss of their families. This poignant tribute records their names etched on bronze strips of 'bark' mounted around the lower section of the main trunk of the tree. In low autumn sunshine, Pigeons bask in the reflections from the top surface of each layer of foliage which light up the underside of the layer above, making the whole tree glow with a fire that eclipses the natural colours of the autumn leaves in the avenue of fastigiate trees leading to this monument, in contrast to the stark concrete wall of Tadao Ando's pavilion around the gardens. His sculptural forms seek to create a link between nature and the sky as an essential element in his designs and the curve of the wall evokes the same significance as Libeskind's shards whilst providing perches for Doves of Peace.

141

The Dragons of Chinatown are the only active specimens
to be found in Manchester. The resident guardians of
Chinese culture maintain a presence throughout the year,
ready to protect occasional visitors and prepare for the
New Year celebrations in traditional style.

AIR
WATER
EARTH
FIRE

Another World

The house of the Apothecary Thomas Minshull stands in
Cateaton Street, adjacent to the Hanging Bridge. This
was the principal approach from the town to the Collegiate
Church, now the Cathedral, where he was buried in 1698.
The house, founded in 1689, was bequeathed to Trustees
'to apprentice poor sound & healthy boys of Manchester
in honest labour & employment'. It was rebuilt in 1890.

Many Apothecaries set up their businesses in one lane in the town, called Phoenix Street because the signs outside their shops displayed an image of the fabulous Arabian bird. Some hung up devices like the one described by Shakespeare in Romeo's desperate search for the Apothecary's shop in Mantua which sounds so much like the mystical interiors of this cluster of medieval shops in Manchester:

> 'And in his needy shop a tortoise hung,
> An alligator stuff'd, and other skins
> Of ill shaped fishes; and about his shelves
> A beggarly account of empty boxes,
> Green earthen pots, bladders and musty seeds,
> Remnants of pack thread, and old cakes of roses
> Were thinly scattered to make up a show'.

And who can deny that the Apothecaries were showmen? When the New World was discovered, they quickly introduced adventurous alligators to replace the crocodiles, unfamiliar reptiles endowed with quasi-religious significance which had been brought back by pilgrims from the Holy Land. These mysterious symbols were supposed to convince customers that Apothecaries could work miracles, turn base metals into gold or dispense the secret of eternal life. Those who could not afford an alligator or a second-hand crocodile were obliged to use painted signs because a stuffed Phoenix was extremely hard to find? The Night Light Company's production of 'Romeo and Juliet' at the Contact Theatre characterised the Apothecary himself as a Phoenix in the form of a large puppet operated by several actors to give it mystical animation.

145

According to Greek legends, when the Phoenix came to the end of its life it built a nest incorporating aromatic spices and resins, just like those in the Apothecary's shop. This became a funeral pyre on which it died, singing a melodious dirge as a new life arose from the ashes. So the Phoenix became known as the 'Firebird' and in the 2010 Manchester Day Parade it became a symbol of the amazing ability of Manchester to turn any disaster into an opportunity to reinvent itself. A Phoenix with wings covered in feathers representing flames, was brought to life by skilled artists manipulating this colourful bird with larger-than-life movements. In 2011, another Phoenix had the same fiery colours with a leaner, prehistoric character and a more determined gliding movement. In 2012, yet another reincarnation was mounted on a mechanical contraption with levers which articulated its head, beak and wings with their red and gold metallic plumage. This bird had a family of Phoenix chicks marching behind it in the same plumage, some on foot, some on stilts and some on unicycles, celebrating the Carers of Manchester, expressing the tenacity of Mancunians in the most optimistic manner.

Because of its ability to produce a new life from the ashes, the Phoenix was adopted by Christians as a symbol for the Resurrection. It is featured on the altar cloth in the Regimental Chapel in the Cathedral, rising from a crescent of embroidered flames beneath the orange glow of the Fire Window designed by Margaret Traherne and installed in 1966 to commemorate the 50th anniversary of the Battle of the Somme and the bombing of the Cathedral in the Blitz of 1940. This Chapel was dedicated to the memory of those lost in War, and the Phoenix's commitment to regenerate life from the flames inspires hope for the future, not only in a military context but also as a challenge to the citizens of Manchester who always respond to this with a great deal of imagination.

Any search for evidence of a Phoenix in Manchester would naturally lead in the direction of places where fire is an essential component of an industrial process. So a visit to a foundry where they cast objects from molten metal brought up to fearful temperatures in crucibles might be a possible nesting place for the bird? However, the Phoenix Foundry in Piercy Street, like all the industry in the Ancoats area, has disappeared and was clearly not able to work the same magic as the Phoenix to achieve its own resurrection. In fact, the foundry had already embarked on a second life within the old Phoenix Cotton Mill but this has since been demolished. Its name lives on in the collection of outbuildings which survive next to the Beswick Street Bridge over the Manchester and Ashton Canal. These have been adapted to house the Osteopathic Centre for Children and the Alzheimer's Society, and whilst this new function undoubtedly seeks to bring new life to the people afflicted with these conditions, further resurrection involving either Fire or the intervention of Apothecaries seems unlikely.

Fossil Record

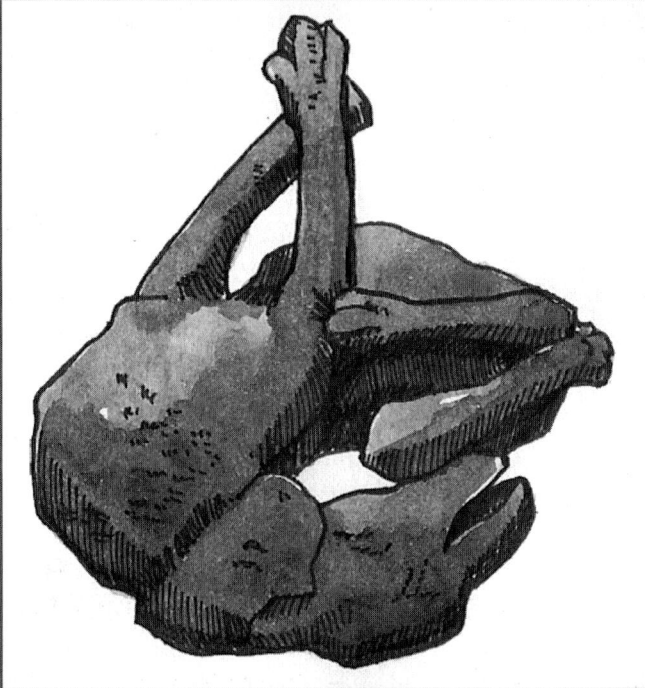

Natural disasters are illustrated in the Living World Gallery in the Manchester Museum; volcanoes and earthquakes are more powerful than anything which man has invented. Pyroclastic debris could smother surrounding areas more quickly than evacuation could be arranged, trapping people and household pets beneath layers of suffocating ash.

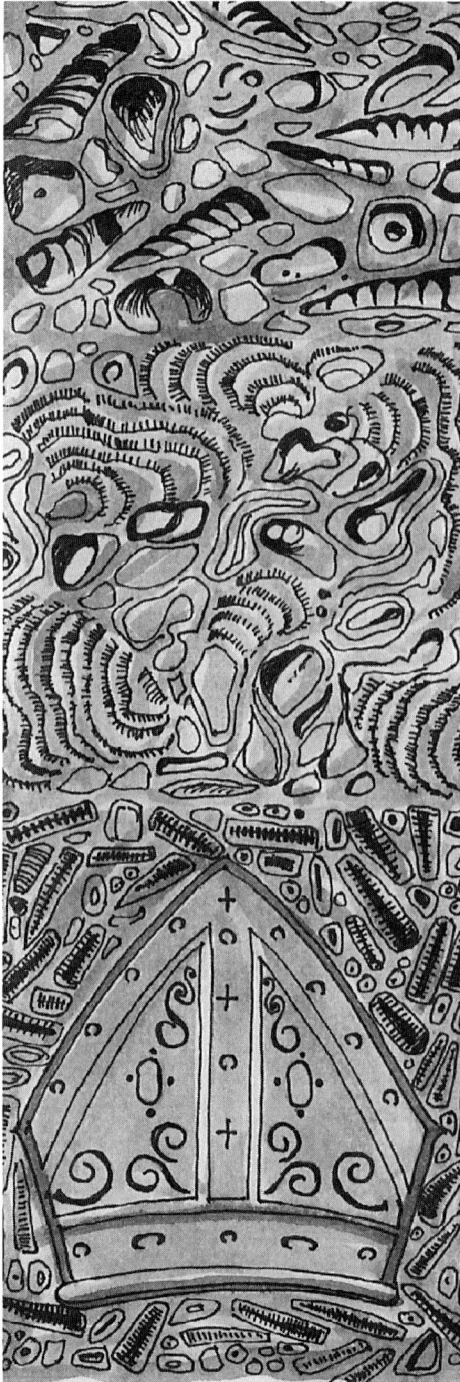

The Romans invaded Britain in AD43 and established a fort at Mamucium in AD79, the same year in which Mount Vesuvius erupted, obliterating Pompeii and Herculaneum. News of this natural disaster would eventually have reached the occupying army on the edge of the Empire where legionaries would have learned the fate of families left behind. Unlike collateral casualties of war, the bodies of people and their domestic animals engulfed by volcanic ash became like fossils as they decayed within the debris which quickly set into rock. Almost two thousand years later, archeologists made the plaster casts to record the evidence of the disaster for visitors to see in Manchester Museum. A much longer natural process trapped fossils of turrilites, goniabasts, crinoids and tiny organisms in the limestone deposits laid down in the Jurassic period, carried miles away from any sea by the movements of Earth's tectonic plates which define geological time. These would be hewn from quarries in the 20th century to clad modern office buildings in Mosley Street and Portland Street, and the Crown Courts in Spinningfields; the stone paving inside Manchester Cathedral, removed to allow installation of a new heating system, was quarried in Derbyshire. Man has become so adept at moving things around the globe that future archeologists, discovering remains of Manchester beneath desert sands somewhere in the northern hemisphere millions of years hence, will have a more complex set of stories to unravel.

Shades of Grey

The chancel of Manchester Cathedral contains choir stalls decorated with one of the finest collections of medieval misericords in England. Made between 1485 and 1506, those on the north side were paid for by a prosperous merchant, Richard Beswick, whose arms are carved on the north-east stall end. The carvings on the seats tell their own story - which is open to interpretation.

Our text today is taken from the First Epistle of Paul to Timothy, Chapter 6 verses 9 and 10: *But they that will be rich fall into temptation and a snare, and into many foolish and hurtful lusts, which drown men in destruction and perdition. For the love of money is the root of all Evil.* This sums up the lamentable condition in which we find ourselves in the 21st century where the Digital Revolution has eroded the line between Good and Evil. There was a time when representatives of the Church, as instruments of a Higher Authority, enabled those who were poor in education, and thereby also in cash and in time, to make the proper distinction between these polarities of moral standards. Today, the Internet provides information which is no substitute for education whilst it simultaneously absorbs all their time and their money, so people who should be well-educated are, paradoxically, momentarily cash rich and still time poor as a result of their indulgence in hedonistic affluence. So it would seem to be necessary to restore that essential moral difference which allowed simple peasants to work long hours in the fields so that the Lord of the Manor might have time to manage his estates through the equally hard work of hunting and similar arduous tasks well beyond the capacity of the peasants. The peasants would then, in their limited free time, be able to obtain instruction in how to differentiate Good from Evil and learn the penalties that they must suffer should they fail to assimilate such generous education endowed by their Masters. They would learn very quickly that Dragons symbolised the Devil and so could not be trusted. In fact, Dragons were disagreeable creatures who would bite and fight each other. However, the peasants had seen their own dogs teaching their young the techniques of catching prey through play so, naturally, they would ask why should it be considered Evil if Dragons were to do the same? I ask you to consider the nature of the Dragon's prey. Then you will have your answer.

True believers, in their desire to keep to the path of Goodness, depend on the guidance of a trusted protector. Such protection could be acquired by the application of moral principles represented by a Lion, not a live creature, I hasten to add, but a symbolic Lion matched in strength to resist the virtual threat of an Evil Dragon. Of course, that Good Lion would need to be trained very carefully as it is in the nature of the Lion to take every opportunity to seize any unsuspecting prey. But other allies could be called upon to provide support in the timeless struggle between Good and Evil. The 21st century has its virtual images delivered by modern technology but these are nothing more than an interpretation of creatures displayed in the misericords of the Cathedral in the time-honoured fashion of the most primitive cave paintings which were designed to meet the eternal demand for information. They depict the Woodhouses, strange hairy people who lived deep in the forests but, in attempting to make contact with them to enlist their protection, it would be necessary to take considerable risks. They rode curious animals like Camels and Unicorns which they captured through the employment of truly magical powers. For ordinary worldly beings to secure the services of a virtuous Unicorn, it was necessary to tempt it with a Virgin who would bewitch it with her undoubted charms. When the poor creature went all weak at the knees, if you will forgive the expression, it would have no option but to lay its head in her lap and surrender to her commands. The problem that we have to overcome in our current struggles is to recognise that Virgins are now more difficult to find than Unicorns. So the Woodhouses, who were able to capture Unicorns on which to gallop around the forest, must have been a formidable force against Evil, which has always risen up in the weaker souls of Men, as it appears that they were able to work magic powerful enough to charm Virgins?

The surface of the planet which we inhabit is currently covered more by water than dry land and the oceans harboured Serpents because, just like the oceans themselves, Evil is all around us. Tossed on this turbulent Sea of Life, we poor seafarers still need the protection of powerful water-borne Spirits who must be summoned from their shells to purge any Serpents or Dragons lurking in our innermost thoughts, to winkle them out, one might say, to ensure a peaceful and successful voyage whilst engaged in a quest to deliver strange and exotic animals from New Worlds. However, if the Lord of the Manor should contemplate mounting a quest to rid the countryside of Dragons, he would find that his packs of Hounds were no match for these powerful Evil creatures. So he might well have despatched his agents to mount a formidable response and they might have considered employing a war machine of some magnitude. An Elephant, flapping its fearsome ears like the wings of a Dragon, and with the construction of a castle towering on its broad back, would be a sight to strike fear into any opponent. But life for those in more humble positions was difficult in those times and there were many hazards of which peasants needed to be aware in order to avoid being overcome by the forces of Evil. One particular danger was a seven year-old Cock which laid an egg from which would emerge a magical Cockatrice. One look from its Evil eye was enough to instantly strike dead any beholder! So thoughts of all these perils were an incentive to peasants who would be glad to find any diversion from such dangers. They would be grateful to their Masters for allowing them to work hard, leaving them no time to fall into the many traps set about them to capitalise on their human weaknesses. This, after all, was a task to which their Masters had devoted so much of their personal energy and were therefore entitled to any rewards which accrued from such beneficence.

The universal powers of Evil exposed both peasants and their Masters to the same wicked enticements. The peasants might have enjoyed a considerable benefit in having thoughtful Masters to save them from straying into the wrong paths by engaging them in hard physical work, thereby giving them no time to indulge in Evil activities. But what about those Masters on whom they depended for this salvation? They were, after all, human and susceptible to the same fragilities as the peasants. Apart from protecting their personal wealth, a problem from which the peasants were mercifully spared, they were obliged to ensure that they would not yield to idle weaknesses. So they contrived to fill their days with meaningful activities, like hunting Deer with Hounds. This required them to devote much time and attention in training the Hounds to work together to bring down prey much bigger than themselves. Such lessons in co-operation were not wasted as the products of these exercises would grace the Master's table. The irony of this situation was not lost on the peasants who knew that they were likely to be roasted on a spit if the Master were to catch them in possession of so much as a single rabbit they had poached on his land. However, the peasants did not recognise the greater tragedy in their inability to find a way to work together themselves. So to overcome the powers of Evil they were more than willing to accept the encouragement of a Master who distracted them to the point at which they were no longer obliged to think for themselves. Only in their sleep were the peasants allowed to dream their own fantasies of what it would be like if the defenceless victims of all this carnage could turn the tables on those who hunted them. The peasants would never dare to give voice to such thoughts if the Lord of the Manor was in earshot, so they longed for their Master to be disturbed by his own nightmares of being cooked by vengeful Rabbits.

While the peasant dreamed about the vengeance of Rabbits, rather than the retribution of the Lord of the Manor, it wasn't difficult to extrapolate this concept to imagine the irony of a Fox riding a Hound to help him to catch a Hare. This bizarre construct epitomised a world where hunger was a pain familiar to peasants and animals alike and any opportunity to solve the problem would be welcome. It was, therefore, only natural that the Fox should take any chance to steal the odd Goose from time to time and, driven by the extremes of hunger, he would choose his moment when the huntsmen had retired to their Manor to indulge in well-deserved relaxation after a hard day hunting in the field while the peasants were engaged in their own laborious tasks. However, the Fox would still find himself faced with the unavoidable risk of exposing himself to the abuses of the peasant's wife if he attempted to steal her fowl. Then, having caught his meal and fed his family, his work was done, leaving the Fox plenty of time for other things. He appreciated that the Master enjoyed a different status arising from his education so, if the Fox was well-informed, he could pass on his knowledge to his children. Now, if peasants could have done that, what a difference it would have made to their existence! However, the true purpose of a good education must be measured in terms of the ability to organise time. This was beyond the peasants who depended on their Masters to save them from the diversions of life by dictating how they would spend every minute of their working day. On the other hand, the lesson of efficiency was well-absorbed by the ruling classes who set about enclosing all the common land to improve its productivity - and to increase their profits - rather than leave it to the lack of direction of the peasants who were chased from pillar to post and used this as an excuse to protest that their time was no longer theirs to organise so they could hardly accept the blame for their inefficiency.

But there is more to life than achieving efficiency in material terms. In order to take account of the revaluation of moral standards, to move with the times as it were, it is often necessary to redraw the line between Good and Evil. Those on the Good side will point accusing fingers at those on the Evil side, and from time to time it becomes necessary to restore the balance in the clear terms of Black and White by minimising those inconvenient shades of Grey which serve only to confuse the issues. This requires precise definition of the difference between Evil and plain Mischief. In this respect, satirists will take advantage to stray into the Grey areas to ask why the Church should have a monopoly in other creative art forms, like music? It would take a Salvationist to realise that the Devil had all the best tunes, but Pigs dancing to a bagpiper, or playing a harp, must cast doubts as to how much control over the lives of peasants would be considered enough to prevent their straying into the path of Evil? Then the question arises as to where in the scale of Greyness do barbarous sports like Bear-baiting belong? There are those who do not consider this to be a sport at all because, unlike hunting where the quarry has a slim chance to outrun or outwit the Hounds, a tethered Bear stood no chance against a pack of savage Dogs. It was inevitable that the cruel treatment of defenceless animals would, at some point, become unacceptable and the pendulum swung the other way when animals were given Rights. But Rights without Responsibility was not a concept to be easily understood by uneducated peasants and was quite beyond the comprehension of the animals. Some thought that the confiscation of common land from the peasants was nothing short of cruelty, but their Masters always had the responsibility to observe other factors which needed to be taken into account in order to protect the efficiency of the State as executed through the diligence of the Establishment.

The Mosaic commandments included the exhortation that *Thou shalt not steal*, recognising that the solution to poverty is not to be found in stealing from others. It is difficult to persuade uneducated peasants that their security cannot be achieved by the acquisition of wealth but rather in knowing how to conduct life without it. Institutions set up by educated professionals became targets for satirists seeking to challenge their position in the Establishment. But could peasants be trusted to interpret as mere Mischief the subtle nuances of images which suggested that Monkeys were capable of carrying out the work of physicians? Physicians could argue that it was beyond all reasonable doubt that their own training was superior to anything which Monkeys could be taught, if indeed it were remotely possible to teach Monkeys anything? However, the question as to the ability of the physicians' medication to cure all maladies elicited no credible answer as their science, even in the 21st century, is still very much akin to a form of abstract art based upon trial and error. And so it was with all the professions who had to admit to their fallibility - except the money-lenders who somehow managed to work more miracles than all the other professions put together by creating money out of thin air! The alchemists had tried everything they knew to make gold out of base metals, but they failed. Money-lenders, on the other hand, have reduced the entire population to the same status as the Monkeys! Incredibly, no-one ever made the connection that Monkeys could be trained to carry out petty crimes which would put them in the same category as the money-lenders. They believed that in the pursuit of simple theft, any blame could be safely attached to the Monkey rather than its trainer, so should the Monkey's soul be purged if it were to steal from a cheating pedlar? Would the Monkey's trainer need to serve his time in purgatory? Are money-lenders immune from resolving this equation?

As the margins between Good and Evil became blurred with time, power began to slip away from the Church, leaving a vacuum when it came to matters requiring adjudication on issues of conscience in the definition of criminal activities. What account should be taken of the character of anyone accused of indiscretion within this pervasive mist of Greyness? An Eagle perched over a child in a cradle could be assumed to be in the act of taking the child, but could equally be seen to be delivering it so that the Lord of the Manor might pretend that his illegitimate offspring was really a gift from God and common humanity would oblige him to give it shelter. The event might be celebrated as a miracle, as indeed such a stratagem had been spectacularly successful when employed in the Holy Land, so why not in Manchester? Or would a human be guilty of neglect for allowing its child to be kidnapped? Would a Monkey take less care of a kidnapped human baby than one of its own? Would a human be able to take care of an infant Monkey without abusing the defenceless animal if the prospect of financial gain were introduced into the equation? The apportionment of blame became extremely complicated, especially when lawyers saw an opportunity to manipulate their fabrication of laws to enhance their personal financial gain. According to the Psalmists, an Eagle was able to renew its youth, and thereby its Goodness, by plunging three times into a spring of pure water as an analogy to Baptism, because Redemption is not beyond any creature so long as Authority is maintained. So we must return to the premise that the line must be redrawn. The extremes are well enough defined but the centre-ground poses insurmountable questions as to where Good should give way to the Greyness of lesser Evils. Would a bad Master be prepared to cross that line and leave himself open to the admonition of Higher Authorities? Indeed, what or who are the Higher Authorities?

When God's experiment with Creation failed, a Flood was imposed to wash away Evil and its causes. However, one family was spared and thus Man was given dominion over all the beasts of the earth, the creeping things, the fowls of the air and the fish of the sea. This raises the ethical question of whether the scale of Greyness should apply only to Man or must all other creatures comply with the concepts of Good and Evil? We have already observed that the morals of animals are extremely debatable. If some are more pure than others, might this render them capable of lifting themselves out of the mire of Greyness to soar into the rarified atmosphere of the White band? The Pelican must surely be amongst these as, in extreme circumstances, it was believed it would feed its young on its own blood and thereby it symbolises the ritual of the Last Supper and its manifestation in the Holy Communion, at the pinnacle of Goodness at the White end of the spectrum. The evidence for the need to re-establish a canon of universal values is there for all to see in the misericords in the choir stalls of the Cathedral. For long periods they were out of sight of all but the Clergy until democratisation of religion gave access to these images to whoever wishes to construct a contemporary interpretation of the messages contained, thereby removing any suggestion of hypocrisy which might have filtered through the gaps in the spectrum. It is no longer a question of 'do as I say, not as I do' with which parents forever confuse offspring who expect their role models to practise what they preach. Peasants are no more likely to meet the purest Unicorns than they are to encounter the darkest Dragons, so they will be more inclined to accept stories to which they can relate in their own lives. They may know the truth about Pelicans, they might abhor the bestiality of Bear-baiting, they would certainly understand the mischief of Monkeys, but they will feel at home fantasising about musical Pigs!

Here be Dragons

The Chinese Imperial Arch in Faulkner Street, in the heart of Chinatown, is a symbol of power supported by the protection of Dragons. It becomes the focal point of the Chinese New Year celebrations as the Dragon Dancers wind their way from Albert Square to Chinatown.

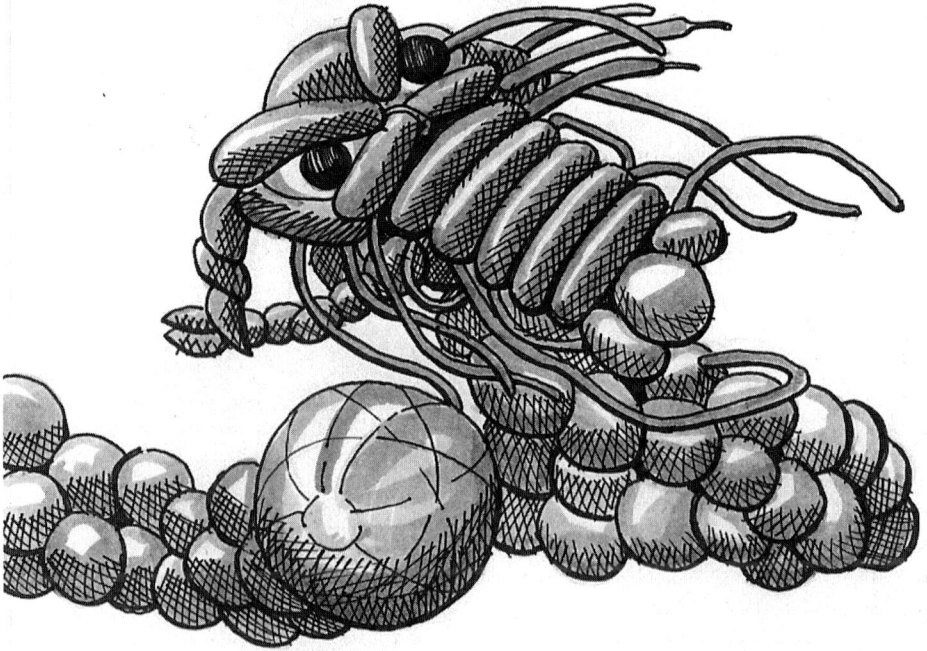

Chinese Dragons are benign creatures, not monsters. We are without wings and earthbound, controlling the water supply, the seas and the rain, a cycle without which life itself would not be possible, even in Manchester. We sit on roof tiles to protect the home or the business below, but the winged European Dragons are a completely different species, breathing fire and living underground, so they are found guilty by association for causing disastrous earthquakes. If that were true, they would deserve their bad reputation but, as nobody has ever seen a Dragon anywhere near an earthquake, the evidence is circumstantial at best and takes no account of the natural mechanisms of the planet. On the other hand, Dragons' ferocity is admirably deployed in our prime task as watchmen who are trusted to guard hoards of golden apples or captive maidens. The Chinese community puts on magnificent New Year celebrations, led by the New Year Dragon with twenty or more operators within its body. It is assisted by several small Lions, visiting businesses, offices, restaurants throughout Chinatown with all the noise of clashing cymbals and booming drums as they dance up the stairs like a thunderstorm with raucous energy to spread their beneficence widely so that no-one is left out. The Manchester Day Parade roused the Dragon from its hibernation to greet the whole city. This Dragon, created from orange and yellow balloons, had a soulful character as it floated without substance, an ethereal presence, rather than a noisy, boisterous creature, spreading its beneficence gently in the sunshine.

Another Chinese tradition is Dragon Boat racing, but Chinatown has no body of open water to suit such activities, so in the best Mancunian spirit to overcome all obstacles, the community invented land-based Dragon Boats. Simple cardboard shells, stiffened by bamboo poles and cable ties, were carried by four runners who transformed the shell into an eight-legged creature with genetic links to the English pantomime Horse, racing around the streets of Chinatown. A new tradition had completed its maiden voyage!

Amorous knights with no wars to fight, turned their thoughts to rescuing maidens from Dragons who were necessarily demonised to justify their quests. The imagination of translators of religious works was applied to exploit allegorical images but confused Dragons with Serpents, calling Satan the 'Great Dragon' in one breath and that 'Old Serpent' in the next. I suppose anything with a long scaly tail was tarred with the same brush. Is that any way to educate people? For the 2011 St George's Day celebrations, the Booth Centre, in collaboration with Mustard Tree under the direction of artist Paul Devereaux, took their inspiration from Mark Cazalet's reredos painting in the Cathedral to create a pair of Giants in a Spanish style. St George became a 21st century young man in an England football shirt cutting the chains of a forlorn Dragon whose passion for the love of his country and his neighbourhood had been imprisoned by apathetic despair. This challenged people to take responsibility for their own short-comings instead of shifting accountability onto some unsuspecting animal in the manner of Aesop. The rain dampened spirits in the 2012 Parade, so the Giants stayed at home to dream of Mediterranean sunshine while their more light-hearted brethren danced amongst the crowds like large cuddly toys so that none of the Knights in Albert Square felt the need to slay them. Real Dragons would have livened up the proceedings.

It would be far better to follow the Chinese recognition of the benign nature of Dragons rather than persist with the uninformed medieval accusations against these and other mythical creatures which inhabit the collection of allegorical images in the Cathedral's misericords. The stories of the Dragon-slayers were equally mythical and reflect the duplicitous character of humans, but without the charm of Aesop's fables. So another job they should have left to real Dragons was the beacon for the Queen's Diamond Jubilee celebrations. Surely Her Majesty was worth a decent bonfire rather than a miserable flame perched on the Cathedral roof like a large Bunsen burner? It might have satisfied the Health and Safety Officer, but if the building had burned down they could have blamed the Dragons? That would have created a job for Dragon-slayers like George and Michael who achieved Sainthood on the strength of one-sided accounts of their exploits. Scapegoats must always be found to take the blame for having done too much of this or too little of that - often both at the same time! The Establishment denigrates the Dragons' alleged capacity to upset the balance of the system while they cause far more devastation through their own global interventions. The general ignorance of the majority of the population is woefully apparent and nothing has changed since the Middle Ages, except that they are now manipulated by Parliament and their puppet-masters rather than the Church. Concepts of Good and Evil have been superseded by the worshipful followers of Mammon who are far more aggressive than any Dragon. Perhaps there is a pattern emerging?

Carvings on medieval buildings confused issues by mixing Evil Dragons with the symbols of Good Evangelists. Eagles, Lions, Oxen and Angels are included at the whim of the stonemason who overlaid the carvings with his own brand of mischief to add to the confusion. These represent no more than a quaint observation on peasants who believed that Gargouille was a great Dragon living in the River Seine and allegedly ravaged 7th century Rouen before the Archbishop claimed that he had 'killed' it. Gargoyle means 'throat', and the spouts which discharged rainwater clear of the building struck fear into beholders looking up to find the source in a grotesque figure with fangs and bulging eyes. The 21st century designers of computer games cast their virtual Dragon-slayers against terrorists in the role of monsters, fabricating a relationship between the 'reader' and the 'subject'. This involves the player as a primitive hunter-killer, justifying the action of killing identifiable Evils on the screen in a virtual world separated from the secure Goodness of family and friends. This 'civilising' effect is expected to fill the vacuum left by a Church which has lost its superstitious claim to authority. Paradoxically, the inspiration for the modern games comes from the same superstitions deployed by medieval craftsmen who decorated buildings with caricatures of Dragons, Demons and mythical animals. So have we really progressed beyond this medieval concept with our modern technology - or do you still not believe in Dragons?

Dragons have become associated with these games in the same way that football teams have adopted various animals as their mascots which take no part in the game but satisfy a primitive belief that they can influence the result of the battle between Good and Evil. Victorian antiquarians studied the details of medieval churches, like Manchester Cathedral, and applied these to revive not so much a style of architecture but the authority of the Established religion. This was in desperate need of reinforcement to combat the attraction of non-conformism to a burgeoning working class who were more easily influenced in the amenable chapels with no intimidating decoration. The John Rylands Library, a temple of scholarship, used the Gothic Revival style, complete with a range of details incorporating disagreeable Dragons, a Phoenix, mythical chimeras like the Griffin, and even a Vampire Bat in an attempt to endow its collection of knowledge with a quasi-religious blessing. Interpretation of information in the books depends on the intelligence of the reader and intelligence has been devalued by the search engines of the internet which provide instant gratification but no depth of understanding. You can't blame that on Dragons, we're only the mascots!

Dragons did their best to occupy the Victorian buildings of Manchester and some of our finest work can be seen in the grotesques which decorate structures that started life as government or commercial offices. These applied the same authority as the Church through architectural means, but there was another battle going on with the Classical Revival style which sought to reflect the power of the Roman Empire in the design of public buildings in a futile attempt to express the expansion of the British Empire. Whichever style was chosen was immaterial because the British Empire very quickly went the same way as the Roman Empire - but the Dragons are still there! However, some references to classical mythology finished up on Gothic Revival buildings which were encrusted with profuse decoration - like ornamental pastry-making? So grotesque creatures appear on the Livebait Restaurant which began life as the Manchester Shipping Offices and Packing Company on Lloyd Street in 1865. Their cousins guard the corners of Katsouris in Deansgate which was originally a government office in 1876 and incorporates a statue of Queen Victoria on its John Dalton Street elevation. Where does Her Majesty fit into the hagiography of Dragons? I don't really think I should ask.

Of all the buildings that really needed to stamp its authority on the population - or those sections of the population who needed to be stamped on - are the Crown Courts in Minshull Street. Thomas Minshull would have appreciated having a street named after him, but there's not an Apothecary's shop in sight. Thomas Worthington who designed the Courts in 1867-73, recognised that he needed to include a few Dragons to do the stamping. However, Earp and Hobbs who did the carving, found a breed of Dragons that were not as intimidating as they might have been. They appear to be vegetarians! How can they intimidate anybody while they sit there on the plinth of the building, eyeball-to-eyeball with those entering its portals, like pet Guinea Pigs chewing the leaves of the foliage which surrounds them? They don't strike fear into the hearts of defendants, so it must be assumed that the designers have abdicated their duties to lawyers who are obviously quite capable of eating miscreants alive - along with anyone else who doesn't give the right answers? Even Dragons struggle to compete with that!

People thought Dragons were too limited in their powers, so they invented new hybrid species with more mettle. The original Chimera of Greek mythology was, according to Homer, a creature with the head of a Lion, the body of a Goat and the tail of a Dragon, like something out of children's books where pages are sliced into three to create amusing mixtures of creatures that don't scare anybody. They tried a bit harder with the Griffin which had the body, tail and hind legs of a Lion with the head and fore legs of an Eagle, looking enough like a Dragon to be sacred to the Sun. Although he had no Dragon in him he was entrusted to guard treasure and is resplendent amongst the fragments of stained glass preserved in the windows of Ordsall Hall. The Wyvern was a winged Dragon with a Serpent's tail, fighting with a Woodhouse in the Cathedral misericords and meeting all the religious criteria to be a diabolical monster whichever way you looked at him. I don't know why he became a symbol for the Kingdom of Mercia, but he finished up on the coat-of-arms of the Midland Railway Company whose lines operated through Mercia and terminated in Manchester Central Station. He took up residence in the Midland Hotel, next to the station, and from there migrated to the Refuge Assurance Company in Oxford Street, now the Palace Hotel. He must have been doing a real Dragon's job of safe-guarding the services of transportation and insurance, in the traditions of medieval heraldry which honoured the Dragon's attributes.

The art of creating hybrids was developed by the cooks in the 16th century kitchens of Ordsall Hall, presumably inspired by the stained glass? They couldn't find a Lion or an Eagle in the market so they sewed together the front half of a small pig and the rear half of a large chicken, proving that Mancunian necessity is the mother of invention. They called it a 'Cockentrice' which sounds uncomfortably like the deadly Cockatrice of the medieval carvings in the Cathedral, but this half Fowl, half Pig with an apple in its mouth, was difficult to take seriously even if it was good to eat. The tradition lives on in the work of artist, Banksy, whose graffiti on the Tib Street substation was discovered in 2009. He designed an animal with a Lion's head and mane attached to a Dog's body with a tail trimmed in the style of a Poodle. Extrapolation of these characteristics defies analysis unless some mysterious electrical power from the substation has been harnessed? Banksy calls his work 'Street Art' with an essentially transient nature, so he would not be pleased to find this work has been 'perspexed' and obscured by advertising stickers?

The extremes of the perceived character of Dragons have been illustrated by artists, sculptors, architects and, in all probability, ornamental pastry-makers, in various styles throughout the ages. Properly cherished and nurtured, they will continue to provide service as guardians of the peace of mind for the whole population. There is no longer a need for knights to pretend to slay Dragons because they can buy a knighthood more conveniently these days. If Dragons had been guarding the wealth of the nation, there would have been no financial crisis because they would have chased out the less desirable reptiles whose greed threatened civilisation as we know it. I rest my case.

Till Death us depart

*A reconstruction of a Dinosaur in the Manchester Museum
stands with a small relative in the shadow of the skeleton of
Tyrannosaurus rex. 'King Tyrant Reptile' is the centre-piece
of the gallery which advertises its services as a venue for
marriage celebrations. The vows include the word 'Depart'
which meant to separate effectually in old Prayer Books
and became corrupted to read 'till Death us do part'.*

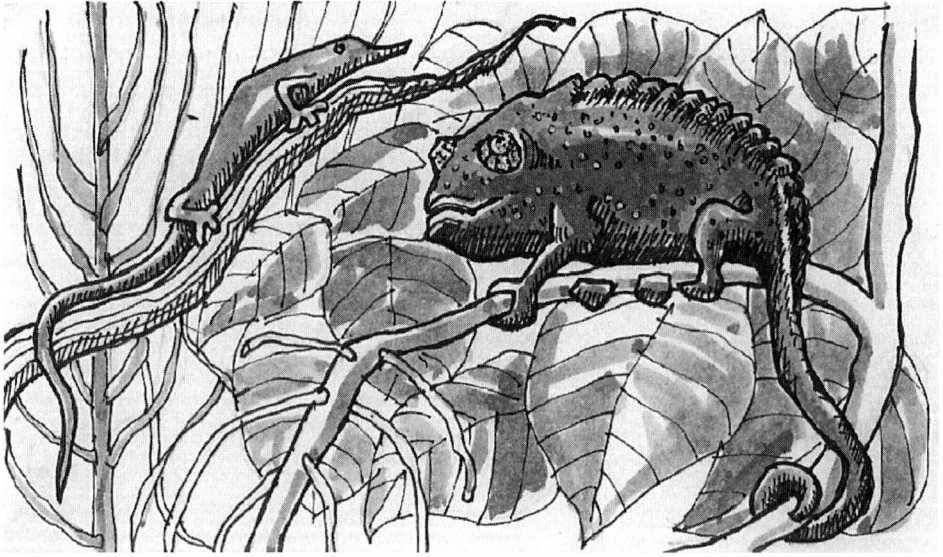

Stan looked forward to the new school term, not that he saw less children during the long summer holidays because they came with their parents who didn't have the same authority as the stentorian schoolteachers. He always looked away when unruly children were taken to one side to be told that it didn't matter how they behaved for their parents at home, but on school trips it was the teacher who was in charge and teachers have rules which will be obeyed. It was the rules that Stan missed, that was it. Even when children kept to the rules, they all seemed to have just as much fun, charging about with their clipboards, ticking boxes, completing puzzles, searching for clues in the cabinets. By the time they reached Stan, they had already been through the Egyptology collection, marvelled at the snakes and lizards in the Vivarium, progressed through the Life Gallery with its cases of butterflies, beetles and bugs. So they had settled down and were well-behaved as they clattered into the Dinosaur hall wearing their archeologists' helmets. Stan was very proud to hear the recital of his statistics and preferred the dimensions to be given in feet because he was an American from South Dakota and they didn't do metric there - certainly not 65 million years ago. They probably didn't do Imperial either but the numbers were bigger and sounded more impressive: 40 feet long, 12 feet high at the hip and 5 feet across the chest. He was especially satisfied when they announced his weight as 6 tons - and he was only 20 years old. What really upset him was being compared to a turkey just because they reckoned he had a 'wishbone' and his feet did look a bit like a bird's. This insult to a *Tyrannosaurus rex* didn't bother the children. They laughed and then immediately forgot because he towered above them and stretched their imagination.

It was a different group which worried Stan. They weren't children but they had clip-boards and ticked boxes and wrote notes with great seriousness - but they had no archeologists' helmets. They were in couples: young men with young women. Some of the young women engaged with another young woman, and an older woman asked lots of questions while the young men stood to one side and looked bewildered. They were all on their best behaviour and the teacher in charge of the group did not have to take anyone aside to explain the rules. "Perhaps it won't be so bad?" Stan hoped. But no-one recited Stan's statistics. Then the teacher talked about 'weddings'. She said they had saved the best until last. "Naturally," Stan thought, "they all did that." The teacher said that weddings were special occasions which united two families who would go on together to celebrate Christenings and Funerals, for ever and ever. Distant cousins, maiden aunts, disreputable uncles would meet each other for the first time - and often the last. With families spread all over the globe, a neutral venue for the nuptials provided a setting in which total strangers could meet each other on equal terms. "Except," Stan insisted, "some of us in here are more equal than any of those puny specimens listening to the teacher". She explained how the Dinosaurs would contribute a background which would occupy the attention of even the most disinterested guest who would go away with unforgettable memories of the occasion.

172

Stan snorted in disgust. "So I've been hanging around for 65 million years just to divert the attention of some bored wedding guest?" That way, the teacher thought, it might be possible to avoid incidents which would be more difficult to forget. "Over my dead body!" Stan could hardly contain himself. As soon as they had all gone, Stan could hear a buzz of excited conversation coming from the Jurassic section. He strained to catch what was going on and he gathered that the idea of 'weddings' had inspired some of the inmates of the gallery to think of regularising their own cohabitation arrangements. The elegant Pliosaur was peering round the column to catch the eye of his beloved neighbour, the Ichthyosaur. He dreamed of seeing her generous form floating down the concourse of the gallery, attended by her colourful armada of Ammonites as bridesmaids. He thought Stan could be the 'best man', or would his impressive stature make him more suited for the role of 'celebrant'? "Do you, *Maeroplata longirostris*, take *Stenopterygius acutirostris* to be your lawful wedded wife?" They were rehearsing the ceremony already. "Stop this nonsense!" Stan yelled and sulked on his plinth. He wondered why their vows couldn't be witnessed by the mummified Pharaohs or the taxidermists' masterpieces - or even the swivel-eyed chameleons? "Anywhere but here. I will lose all credibility if they do it here! What would the children think if they find that a meat-eating theropod, a 'King Tyrant Reptile', is no longer awesome!? That would be worse than being called an over-sized turkey!"

Tail Piece

Waterhouse's Town Hall is a work of poetry without words, celebrating Manchester with images linking the industry of the city to its prosperity. Myriad illustrations of botanical motifs in stone, tiles, glass, metalwork and painted decoration culminate in the celebrated murals by Ford Maddox Brown lining the Great Hall like an epic poem evoking two thousand years of history.

Saint Saëns, in his 'Carnival of the Animals', included fine specimens known as Pianists who, according to poet Wendy Cope, should not be fed sugar lumps but given only applause when you're quite sure they've finished. So a Manchester Menagerie would not be complete without its own fine specimens known as Poets, creatures with fire in their bellies, passion in their words and determination to record for posterity the wonders of their world, its conflicts, its characters and its contradictions. Their finely crafted observations challenge audiences by holding up a mirror to their lives, safeguarding civilisation with the staunchness of Dragons, their words inhabiting buildings like spirits who can be called up to recount their experiences. Sometimes the architecture itself evokes the memories but Poets leave eternal words whilst the Great and the Good are fossilised in marble statues. The annual Manchester Literature Festival celebrates Poetry readings and book signings at venues all over the city, from the Royal Exchange to the City Library, from the Martin Harris Centre in the University to the Cornerhouse. In 2012, a walk around the city centre examined 'Poems of the City' in buildings which echo with the thoughts of Poets on events that shaped the last two centuries. A statue of Abraham Lincoln presides over Brazennose Street connecting the driving force of Cottonopolis with this champion of the anti-slavery movement which established solidarity between the Southern States and Manchester when the Civil War cut off the supply of raw materials to the city's cotton mills. William Cowper's 'Negro's Complaint' acknowledges the plight of the slaves on the plantations in 1788. Walt Whitman added poems to his collection 'Leaves of Grass' and was dismissed from his post as editor of the Brooklyn Eagle for his anti-slavery editorials. His poetry responded to Emerson's argument that the Poet should become 'a liberating god'. On the site of the Free Trade Hall, the fate of demonstrators at the events of Peterloo in 1819 at the hands of drunken cavalrymen is lambasted by Shelley in his satirical tirade 'Masque of Anarchy'. The presence of the Working Men's Church and Street Children's Mission in Spinningfields, cheek by jowl with affluent retail fashion outlets, reminds us that the poor are ever with us and their condition is narrated by John Cooper Clarke in 'Beezley Street' which demonstrates that the Victorian concept of private wealth and public squalor is no longer alleviated by philanthropists. The Midland Hotel shares its heritage with the adjacent railway terminus in W H Auden's 'Night Mail'. Across St Peter's Square at the Cenotaph, Wilfred Owen, who was commissioned into the Manchester Regiment, is remembered for his lament, 'Dulce et Decorum Est', describing the horrors of a gas attack in trench warfare where 'the Poetry is in the pity' and the thoughts of Homer on the honour of dying for one's country have little meaning. The Poet Laureate, Carol Ann Duffy, introduces dark humour in her 'Valentine', comparing love to an onion with its many tearful layers, whilst the John Rylands Library in Deansgate is filled with layers of literature without the tears.

With so many opportunities to link the work of living and dead poets to the history of the city, there is inspiration for a new generation to emerge with fires kindled by the sparks of imagination from the Centre for New Writing at the University of Manchester and from the Creative Writing courses of the Manchester Metropolitan University. The students take part in events at the Literature Festival and in Carol Ann Duffy's evening celebrations of the spoken word at the Royal Exchange Studio where they can read their work in the company of established guest Poets with intermissions of jazz and conversation. At the same time as Carol Ann Duffy was appointed Poet Laureate, Liz Lochhead became Makar of Scotland. She brought her musical Scots dialect to this venue, reading Robert Burns's *'To a Mouse, On turning up in her Nest with the Plough, November, 1785'*, together with her response *'From a Mouse'* which suggested that it was the Ploughman who really took centre stage? And who is to take centre stage in the Menagerie? Poets are like all the other creatures, vying for position as King of the Urban Jungle, presenting their personal view of the world about them.

The Poet Laureate herself, at home in the Manchester Metropolitan University lecture theatre, gave pleasure to many children and their parents reading her story, '*The Princess' Blankets*', to a backdrop of its magical illustrations by Catherine Hyde and with music by John Sampson playing on a variety of period instruments. In the 2012 Literature Festival, her performance in the Banqueting Room of the Town Hall, with the LiTTLe MACHiNe setting well-known poems to music, was worthy of much more than applause - or even sugar lumps. She observed that the Government was withdrawing funds for the arts because of financial crises caused by waging unwinnable wars, by corrupt banking systems, by detached politicians who have no soul. They made token funds available for the 'Cultural Olympics' as a sideshow to their populist promises to support the non-creative activity of sport as a 'legacy' of the Olympic Games. Carol Ann Duffy's poem for that occasion could not let it pass without comment on the institutions which caused the austere conditions that have been imposed on the whole population. This Poet Laureate might be Queen Bee but she has a waspish sting in her tail. So is the position of the Poet Laureate, like the medieval Court Jester within the Establishment, accorded the same immunity from those who cannot acknowledge the presence of the bare truth here or simply cannot bear to hear the truth?

Carol Ann Duffy's predecessor as Poet Laureate was Sir Andrew Motion who delivered his 'Manchester Sermon' in the Cathedral for the 2011 Literature Festival. Like John Keats, he believed that Poets are chameleons who implicate their audience in a moral universe balanced between knowing and not knowing, recognising but questioning, obliging them to tell truths by surprising means to illuminate the experience of what it means to be human, so their poetry should say more of the Poem and less of the Poet. Language is constantly shifting so poetry's appeal must adapt to changes in the complicated rhythms of that language and the meanings of words. He argued that Poetry, like Prayer, gives spiritual value to words, and the King James Bible, designed to be heard in the same way as Shakespeare's plays which were created at the same time, enabled ploughmen to be as well-informed as priests. He raised awareness in his audience to the actions of the Philistines who don't know the price of anything so have no idea of the value of the arts and their capacity to sustain people's lives or reconcile day-to-day conflicts around us. Keats declared that 'the Poetry of the Earth is never dead' and Man, having assumed dominion over that Earth, must put Fire into that Poetry.

The Green Room was an early Mancunian casualty caused by maladministration of financial institutions. With hardly any notice, it lost all funding for its programme of anarchic events of poetry, experimental theatre, burlesque, cabaret and creative activities which do not fit into a comfortable pigeonhole. The Green Room didn't exactly burn down, but it left no ashes from which to rise, Phoenix-like, to begin a new life. However, before it closed its doors, it turned up the heat to give the melting-pot of Manchester a final stir, incorporating ingredients from all over the world as international visitors came to forge cultural links through the spoken word. A quartet of Black Writers presented a collection of poems, 'When Black is Red', for the 2010 Literature Festival: Seni Seneviratne, John Lyons, Peter Kalu and Grace Nichols all wore something red to keep the Fire alive. Another writer of West Indian origin, Poet Kei Miller, combined Poetry with Art at the Whitworth Gallery. He delivered letters in his warm Caribbean tones responding to David Hockney's series of prints of his experiences in 1960s New York inspired by William Hogarth's 18th century series 'The Rake's Progress'. At the City Art Gallery, Nigerian artist, Jalili Atiku, described how he made himself into an installation of placards in Lagos asking 'why are we being punished for your inefficiencies?', expecting arrest at any time. English freedom of speech allows such questions but imposes no obligation on Government to provide answers, removing all hope of remedial action.

The Contact Theatre, well-known for experimental work in all forms of performing art, has produced material which appeals to young generations who are deeply involved in social, political and multicultural issues. Akiel Chinelo, winner of the 1996 Poetry Slam competition, developed his skills through his thoughtful and measured performance of *'Doin' Moon'*. Finely crafted sequences of poetic correspondence took place between Scorcha, a prisoner doin' moon in his cell, and his classical cello wife, played by Anwen Lewis, waiting for his return home. The nuances of human relationships and the deep emotions explored in this symbiosis between the spoken word and music, dealt with all aspects of incarceration and separation, from tender revelations to utter frustration. Another link between music and poetry was a fictional drama *'Beat Surrender'* by Brian Clarke and Tom Elliot at the RNCM. An unsettling encounter between Beat Poet Jack Kerouac and a couple about to be married obliged them to make decisions which fragmented their memories as they peered into the abyss of space between moments of time which stood still. They didn't realise that lives can change in a beat if people allow themselves to take advantage of that window of opportunity. Most people are never aware of those precious moments. After the performance, members of the cast read their favourite Kerouac poems to simulate a Beatnik 'happening'.

Telling truths by surprising means can be achieved by presenting them as fiction to detach them from the bias of propaganda peddled as truth by 'factual' news items and documentaries. Writers from conflict zones around the world, particularly the Middle East, brought their own experiences of conflagration to the International Anthony Burgess Foundation. Mansoura Ez Eldin, Kamel Riahi and Youseff Rakha discussed their work in the context of the 'Arab Spring' which inspired oppressed people to harness the power of the imagination to do what had always seemed impossible to them. They described their individual experiences in Egypt, Tunisia and Algeria and concluded that, after removing tyrants, too much corruption had robbed them of trust and the resources to be able to move forward. The only thing people had left was hope, but before their 'revolution' they had no hope - so some progress has been made - and Poets are in the front line. The opening of the Burgess Foundation, located appropriately in the Engine House of Chorlton New Mills in Cambridge Street, generated a rise in the literary temperature with performances by writers having connections to Manchester. Howard Jacobson presented his novel 'The Finkler Question' which went on to win the Booker Prize. He valued the live presentation rather than spreading the word through the internet which he insists 'does not do satire, essays or thought', so it was hardly surprising that some of his answers to questions provided a stimulating amount of serendipity and his incendiary language records events in the same spirit as Poets.

As part of the Manchester Literature Festival in 2011, Julian Daniel hosted the Poetry Slam Championships at the Yard Theatre in Hulme, bringing together winners surviving from preliminary heats of performance poetry around the region. Finalists, each competing for the critical acclaim of a panel of celebrity judges and members of the audience, presented highly polished personal observations of the human condition with an acoustic language unlike that of the voices of Poets Laureate. Poets of every size, shape, colour and texture delivered time-limited presentations with super-charged passion in character and content, demonstrating that they have absorbed the worst that life can throw at them and can manipulate this through their craft. Some surprised their listeners in more subtle ways than others. The winner of an extremely tense competition was Mark Mace Smith who brought the evening to a dramatic conclusion, assaulting his audience with his heated political party piece of a satirical voice accompanied by beat box effects of two virtual turntables, inflaming his thoughts. This exploited the rhythms of street language of the day to reach out to an audience who see Poetry as a spectator sport and would not be moved by classical poetic forms.

Urbis was reopened in 2012 as the National Football Museum but has retained the vital aspect of its former existence as a centre of excellence in presenting works of art with political and social themes. Its exhibition space presented *'Moving into Space'* as its first major art installation. Albeit football-related, this linked with the *'We Face Forward'* celebration of art from West Africa across the city in exhibitions at the City Art Gallery, the Whitworth Gallery and the Gallery of Costume. As part of this event, Mark Mace Smith delivered a poetry workshop using the artwork as a stimulating backdrop. Audience participation in some of his wicked rhymes was an invitation for younger members of the group to use some milder Anglo-Saxon words they probably wouldn't use in front of their parents, giving a different interpretation to the dimension of surprise advocated by Sir Andrew Motion. As a hook to get young people interested in the rhythm and sound of colourful language, they were a useful tool to engage attention, but came dangerously close to the boundary of acceptability for a young audience. A more appropriate - and safer - approach was his use of a small djembe drum to identify the onomatopoeic rhythm and sounds of long words, linking this to his beat box style. Poets must always be prepared to push the boundaries as part of their very existence.

On UNESCO's World Poetry Day, Matt Panesh/Monkey Poet, launched his first 'Spoke 'N' Heard' poetry night in the Live Room above Gullivers in Oldham Street with the aim of bringing performance poetry to a whole new audience. His piece on the attributes of St George, delivered at scorching speed, listed all the causes for which the Saint is patron, from farmers, scouts and soldiers to Malta, Portugal and syphilis, with much more in between, before drawing the conclusion that a Saint with such a mastery of patronage is ideal for England with its superior attitude to just about everything? His first guest was Mark Mace Smith with more of his observations on the human condition, audience participation rhymes and his immaculate human beat box. On another occasion it was John Hegley who brought his own style of surprising rhymes to the proceedings. However, he had surprised himself by locking his keys inside his home and before he could attend the evening gathering, he was obliged to buy new underpants, borrow a mandolin and change his presentation when he found he was unable to obtain a copy of his book 'Uncut Confetti' in Manchester and his new work had not been released to bookshops. The account of this chain of events provided entertainment enough for his audience but their involvement in his piece '(Unbridled) Guillemot'

> turned them into a very silly lot
> flapping arms so they couldn't stand still a lot
> as they found his style somewhat chilli-hot
> but if I carry on, I shall fill a lot ... more pages?

John Hegley doesn't exactly blaze on stage but he smoulders with the intense heat of a garden barbeque, grilling his poetry and his audience alike. In 2010 he opened the Graduation exhibitions of the Manchester School of Art in the Holden Gallery with his personal blend of poetic humour and audience participation. He returned in 2011 to present an evening of performance poetry at the Martin Harris Centre in the University of Manchester as part of an educational project with local schools and students of the Metropolitan University. The resulting material, some of which he included in his presentation, he dedicated to 'people with teaching difficulties' and I don't think he meant those struggling with the Class from Hell! A stream of poetic riddles, bilingual stories, songs about his 'Luton Bungalow' and a gentle roasting to humiliate late-comers who blamed their sat-nav equipment for their tardiness, flowed seamlessly to send the audience home with a warm glow. He is a Chimera of a performer being part Poet, part Musician and part Comedian, somewhere between a dependable Griffin and a deadly Cockatrice? But what should he be called?

Only yards from Gullivers on Oldham Street is a venue tucked away in a former shop in Afflecks Palace. The Three-Minute-Theatre, 3MT, is an embryo Green Room seeking to provide an outlet for new and experimental theatre, comedy, film, music, burlesque - and Poetry. Mark Panesh performed his theatrical piece *'History Lesson: Welcome to Afghanistan'*, an adaptation of the memoire of Lt John Greenwood from 1844 as an account of the apparently random decisions of British military and political leaders which ended as a complete folly. The experience left him with the hope that this will never, never, never happen again. Perhaps it won't? He also presented a new work of a literary murder mystery as a preview to its introduction at the Edinburgh Festival in 2012 along with more of his poems. On another occasion he introduced Richard Tyrone Jones who celebrated his heart failure at the age of 30 as a presentation of poetry with anecdotes of his experience of 'cardiomyopoetry', sitting on a high stool in front of a screen on which he projected animated backgrounds of hospital wards behind him and cut-away sections of his heart on his t-shirt. Entitled *'Big Heart'*, this won acclaim at the Edinburgh Fringe, so his heart was obviously in the right place. The intimacy of this space is ideally suited to poetry and other creative work where the performance moves imperceptibly into a discussion which becomes a social gathering.

The Portico Library opened in 1806 and its subscribers included Unitarian minister Rev William Gaskell, who was Portico's Chairman for 35 years. However, his wife, Elizabeth Gaskell, could not become a member as women were excluded from such indulgence. It is possible that Charles Dickens might have visited the elegant reading room as their guest, so to commemorate the bicentenary of the author's birth, the Library launched a book of poems by various writers as responses to his life, characters, plots or settings from his novels and entitled 'Our Mutual Friend'. John Hegley's contribution begged Mr Dickens not to 'tell us Nancy's tale tonight'. Like Dickens, Poets record the details of life's experiences to remind us that we live in a cycle in which events have a frightening habit of repeating themselves. The sedate presentation at the Portico was a reflection of the audience, many of whom were of mature years with a sprinkling of academics, people who are never stuck for the right word and have no need to resort to gratuitous expletives but can surprise an audience with imagination. Not for them the street language and beat box rhythms, and certainly not the open-mic sessions which attract attention-seeking performers who would not pass Andrew Motion's test because they still have to learn that Poetry is a celebration of language and not a mutilation of manners so long as their work says more about the Poet than the Poems.

Artists constantly produce work around the city in various media of literature, art, film, drama, music, architecture - and cake decoration - some solidly monumental, others fleeting performances. Lemn Sissay's unique form of performance Poetry lives on in typographical installations which have become landmarks because they communicate directly with the people of Manchester. Amongst the traffic lights on Oxford Road, his words 'Rain' down the gable end of a kebab shop and assure us that 'Harvey's Well' in Rusholme. He catches 'Numbers' at the Shudehill Bus Station and, most recently, his appeal to 'Let there be peace' was unveiled in the atrium of the University Centre. His thoughts flow along the course of the River Tib from New Cross to Market Street but, like the river, it is disappearing as the installation disintegrates under the repeated battering from barrels trundling into the clubs and bars along its route. This work is so loved that there are proposals to resite it where traffic is lighter and in a form more able to resist destruction because we need constantly to remind those whose eyes are fixed on the ground to think about life before it, too, disappears down the cracks between the 'Flags'.

The Olympic Games enlisted Lemn Sissay to provide a poem to encase one of the electrical transformers supplying power to the site. His piece 'Spark Catchers' was an incendiary recollection of life in the Bryant and Mayes Match factory which had previously occupied the site, developing explosive thoughts around the meanings of the word 'strike'.

LIKE US THEY HOLD
THE PEOPLE OF A
MODERN EARTH
THIS WORLD
BETWEEN THE
WINDSWEPT FLAGS

The Town Hall's collection of sculpture, murals and other installations celebrate the industry, arts and sciences which made the city. It hosts literary events, music and performances, including resurrecting the ghosts of the Tib Street pet shops in 'The Birds' by Frolicked for the 2012 History Festival when children and their parents followed a trail of clues around the building to gather items to entice the elusive Rubius harmonius to build a nest. However, there is no reference or any permanent celebration in the building as a visual record of the contribution which so many Poets have made to the cultural life of Manchester.

Creative energy of the city bubbles up everywhere and is particularly evident in the Northern Quarter where imaginative artists, designers and *fashionistas* harness the craft traditions and history of the area to inspire their activities. Ephemeral graffiti sit alongside the more sustainable poetry installations of Lemn Sissay. Stewy's image of the Salford-born punk Poet, John Cooper Clarke, presided briefly over the ironicons in the Oldham Street pavement, immortalising his record *'Disguise in Love'*. Stewy also stencilled a menagerie of British native fauna on the gable end of the Wheatsheaf pub, the bar of Gullivers, building site hoarding in Tib Street, shutters of Vinyl Revival in Hilton Street and a shop in Stevenson Square. This has not created an Urban Jungle but a piece of rural England come to seek its fortune in the city, reviving Romantic concepts of 18th century picturesque traditions when classical Roman ruins were reconstructed as Italian Renaissance features in landscape design and architecture - and in Poetry. There is an Italian proverb that believes that 'the tongue of a Poet is always the last to be corrupted'. Manchester must be the least corrupt city in the Kingdom?

Response to the environment requires determination,
But technology can circumvent the best imagination.
The mobile phone's a Shaman controlling all freewill
Of those in thrall to Mammon on a road that's all downhill.

Games designers make them hungry for virtual experience
And fill their live reality with suspect zombie aliens.
Set these aside and write your thoughts in tactile hardback book,
Drawing pencil lines on pads, awed when you begin to look.

By joining dots the light will dawn, surprises are revealed
Without clandestine robots whose aims remain concealed.
Now sever all connection from techno-tyranny
And find a new direction - discover Poetry!

Acknowledgments

I am fortunate to live in the midst of the myriad major institutions of Manchester whose permanent collections and visiting exhibitions have provided so much inspiration for this project. I am grateful to the Imperial War Museum North, Manchester City Art Gallery, Manchester Museum, Manchester Science and Industry Museum, Ordsall Hall, People's History Museum, Portland Basin Museum and Whitworth Art Gallery where I have gathered images of items as a basis for my drawings.

I am also grateful to Blank Space Gallery, Chinese Arts Centre, Contact Theatre, Cornerhouse, Craft and Design Centre, CUBE, International Anthony Burgess Foundation, John Rylands Library, Library Theatre, Manchester Metropolitan University, Manchester Town Hall, Royal Exchange, RNCM, University of Manchester, Victoria Baths and the Yard Theatre, Hulme, whose buildings, temporary exhibitions and live performances have added many images to my sketchbooks.

My thanks to the Dean and Chapter of Manchester Cathedral and, in particular, to Canon Andrew Shanks for his observations and helpful information regarding details of the building.

Reference has been made where possible in the text to individual artists, architects, poets, writers, musicians and ornamental pastry-makers. My thanks to them all and to the organisers of the various Festivals in which they took part.

Thanks to Wendy Jones of Majolica, Edge Street, for information on the art installations throughout the Northern Quarter on which she worked with lead artist Liam Curtin, commissioned by Manchester City Council with matched funding from the National Lottery, to produce the birds by Adrian Mason, Guy Holden and Helen Kirkpatrick around which 'Dawn Chorus' is based together with additional material by Eve Bennett and Liz Scrine.

To all the businesses, restaurants, pubs, clubs and graffiti artists, many of whom have patiently responded to my mithering in seeking explanations of their signs, logos, window displays, vehicles and other details, for providing me with many 'dots' to join up in my wanderings about the city, I know you were all doing what good Mancunians do but I could not have managed without your help.

The patient staff of Manchester Visitors Information Centre and the City Library have found ways round my reticence to indulge in the internet in searching for background information. Their help has made it possible for a few more dots to be joined up.

And to all those unknown creative people whose presence has added something to this project, my apologies for being unable to acknowledge your individual contributions. To all those people of a delicate disposition, please don't take my satirical observations too seriously. We are all part of a greater entity and cannot be responsible for the fallout caused by those who should know better, but, if we are aware of our environment, we can all do something to stop it being wasted.

Finally, special thanks to Lemn Sissay who insisted that any work on the Zoology of Manchester should include Poets. He was so correct and Anne Beswick's (no relation) inspirational guided walk around the city centre for the Manchester Literature Festival confirmed this.

Bibliography

General

Ashworth, Geoffrey. **The Lost Rivers of Manchester.** 1987.
Bush, Michael. **The Casualties at Peterloo.** Carnegie Publishing Ltd. 2005.
Clottes, Jean. **Cave Art.** Phaidon Press Ltd 2008.
Furuyama, Masao. **Tadao Ando.** Taschen 2006.
Gannaway, C & Jiyoon, L. **Deodorant Type: Sculptures by Gwon Osang.** Manchester Art Gallery 2008.
Hartwell, Clare. **Pevsner Architectural Guides: Manchester.** Penguin Books 2001.
Kellie, Euan. **Rebuilding Manchester.** DB Publishing 2010.
Martin, Sandra. **Adolphe Valette: A French Impressionist in Manchester.** Scala Publishers Ltd. 2007.
Nichols, Robert. **Looking Back at Belle Vue Manchester.** Willow Publishing 1989.
Palmer, Robin. **Dragons, Unicorns and other Magical Beasts.** Hamish Hamilton.
Schofield, J. Ed. **CowParade Manchester Souvenir Guide.** CowParade Manchester Ltd. 2004.
Shanks, Canon Andrew. **Manchester Cathedral.** Scala Publishers Ltd. 2010.
Shelston, Alan. **Elizabeth Gaskell's Manchester.** Gaskell Society 1989.
Silvertown, Jonathan, Ed. **90% Ape: How Evolution Adds Up.** Natural History Museum 2008.
Simpson, M. **Furtive Imagination: Sculpture and Drawings by Nicola Hicks.** Whitworth Art Gallery 1997.
Worthington, Barry. **Discovering Manchester.** Sigma Leisure 2002.

Periodicals

Building Design. **No 601 2nd July 1982: Berthold Lubetkin.**
Northern Voices. **12 Spring/Summer 2011: Frank 'El Ingles' Evans.**

Poetry and Literature

Appelbaum, Stanley, Ed. **Percy Bysshe Shelley: Ode to the West Wind.** Dover Publications Inc, NY1993.
Clarke, Jon Cooper. **Ten Years in an Open-necked Shirt.** Vintage Books 2012.
Dawes, Kwame, Ed. **Red: Contemporary Black British Poetry.** Inscribe/ Peepal Tree Press Ltd. 2010.
Duffy, Carol Ann. **The Princess' Blankets.** Templar Publishing 2008.
Jones, Richard Tyrone. **Big Heart (and other complications).** www.allographic.co.uk 2012.
Loske, Judith. **Sadako's Cranes.** Mine Edition/ Michael Neugebauer Publishing 2011.
LiTTLe MaCHiNe. **Madame Life**. CD by Hotel Zulu Studios 2012.
Morpurgo, Michael. **War Horse.** Kay & Ward Ltd. 1982.
Panesh, Matt. **Monkey Poet's Inappropriate Moral Stories**. Makin Projects Publishing 2011.
Robinson, Peter, Ed. **A Mutual Friend: Poems for Charles Dickens.** Two Rivers Press 2012.
Sissay, Lemn. **Listener.** Canongate Books Ltd 2008.
Stallworthy, Jon, Ed. **Wilfred Owen.** Faber and Faber Limited 2004.
Warren, Celia, Ed. **RSPB Anthology of Wildlife Poetry.** A & C Black 2011 (for JohnHegley: Gillemot)

Italics indicate titles of films, exhibitions, paintings or other works.

Index